Truth Matters

25 Thought-Provoking Essays for
the 21st Century Christian

VICTOR MORRIS

Truth Matters

© 2016 by Victor Morris and Advancing Native Missions

No part of this publication may be reproduced or transmitted in any form or by any means, mechanical or electronic, including photocopying and recording, or by any information storage and retrieval system, without permission in writing from the author or publisher (except by a reviewer, who may quote brief passages and/or brief video clips in a review).

The scanning, uploading and distribution of this book via the Internet or via any other means without the permission of the author or publisher is illegal and punishable by law. Please purchase only authorized electronic editions, and do not participate in or encourage electronic piracy of copyrighted materials.

ISBN: 978-0-9908372-9-9 PAPERBACK

Published by:

Advancing Native Missions
P.O. Box 5303 • Charlottesville, VA 22905
www.AdvancingNativeMissions.com

Graphic Design by:
Christopher & Heather Kirk, GraphicsForSuccess.com

Unless otherwise notated, all Scripture references are taken from the New King James Version®. Copyright © 1982 by Thomas Nelson, Inc. Used by permission. All rights reserved.

For Connie

You have always been such an encouragement to me in my ministry.

I thank God for giving me a sister like you.

Acknowledgements

This book has been years in the making. So it would be impossible to mention everyone who has been involved in its formation. However, there are a number of people who certainly deserve to be mentioned.

Thanks to Virginia Tobias, who despite facing illness and surgery, still took time to edit the manuscript for this book. You are always so patient with me. It is a joy to work with Heather and Christopher Kirk, who did all the layout, design and preparation getting this book ready for printing. Your expertise and enthusiasm are both appreciated. You always do such quality work, despite chronic health challenges. God bless you for your sacrificial effort.

Thanks to David Thacker and the leaders of Advancing Native Missions (ANM). You have approved this project, and encouraged me in my writing endeavors. My work at ANM is focused on a ministry called Truth Builders. I cannot imagine doing this ministry without the Advisory Council of Truth Builders giving me input and advice, holding me accountable, and generally being there in support and encouragement. So thank you to Ruth Graham, Kathy Hassell, Paul Hollifield, Shane Lilly, Joel Maas, Lou Mancari, Dan Reichard, Paul Robbins, and Jay Temple.

How do I express enough gratitude for my wife for all she has done for me and my work. With this project, she read each piece when originally written, editing each one. Then she reread all 25 essays in manuscript form. Sue, your insights and suggestions have made this a much better book. I love you.

Finally, all glory and thanks to the Lord. I know that any talent or ability that I may possess at all is His gracious gift to an undeserving creature.

Table of Contents

Introduction ix
1   *Spiritual Illiteracy* 1
2   *Sizing Up Greatness* 7
3   *Forgive Me, O Great Gaia!* 15
4   *What Evil Lurks in the Hearts of Men* 19
5   *Is Jesus the Only Way?* 27
6   *The Descent of Man* 31
7   *Supermarkets, Sundays and Sanctity* 37
8   *Lords of Misrule* 43
9   *"That's Not Nice!" Good!* 49
10   *Mother Earth Is Only a Child* 55
11   *Here Is Your God!* 65
12   *Is Belief in the Trinity Necessary?* 71
13   *If by Chance…* 77
14   *Does Theology Matter?* 83
15   *The Self-Contradiction of Evolution* 87
16   *Moldy Evolutionary Cake* 91
17   *Have We Lost Our Souls?* 95
18   *Raindrops Keep Falling on Our Heads* 99

19	*Alchemy in the Academy* 103
20	*The Master Artist* 109
21	*Why Doesn't God Destroy Evil?* 115
22	*Peace at All Costs?* 119
23	*An Existential View of Evil* 123
24	*Reason—A Double-Edged Sword* 129
25	*The Dangers of Subjectivism* 133

Topical Index 139

The Ministry of ANM 141

Introduction

"Without absolutes revealed from without by God Himself, we are left rudderless in a sea of conflicting ideas about manners, justice and right and wrong, issuing from a multitude of self-opinionated thinkers."
–John Owen (1616-1683)

It all began with snow. It was April of 2001. I was living in Markleysburg—a small community in the mountains of southwest Pennsylvania. It had been a long, cold, and very snowy winter. Indeed, the snow seemed interminable. It just would not quit.

On April 4, I awoke to see yet another snowstorm. By the time I got to the church where I was working, I was fed up. I was once an avid fan of snow, but I had had enough. In my frustration I quickly penned a small rant on the evils of snow that I called "Thoughts on White Stuff." Hoping that venting my irritation to others would help alleviate some of my snowbound misery I emailed this short essay to various friends and family. I was surprised by the response. Several people wrote that they enjoyed my writing, and encouraged me to write more. So I began a series of email messages that lasted for several years. At one time I was emailing about 80 people these pieces. (This was obviously in the pre-blog era.) I called the series "Trogo," a Greek word that means to chew or to ruminate. The idea was that I wanted to provide people with "something to chew on," i.e., thoughts to ponder. These pieces were sometimes serious, sometimes silly. They dealt with current events, philosophical musings, theology, contemporary culture and apologetics. Basically whatever was banging around in my head made it to the computer keyboard.

Fast forward a few years. I moved from PA to Virginia to work at an interdenominational missions agency called Advancing Native Missions (ANM). After six years of working in various capacities at ANM, in 2012 I felt led of God to start a ministry initiative for ANM called Truth Builders Ministries. Truth Builders is a resource for both the domestic church in the U.S. and ANM's international ministry partners. This ministry deals with apologetics, Bible doctrine, cults, world religions, the occult and worldviews. As part of this effort we started a blog in 2013. The Truth Builders blog offered posts on various cults and false teachings. It also answered people's questions on the Bible and the Christian faith. In addition, it was a typical blog, with my observations on various issues and topics. That part was essentially Trogo reborn. Again, much to my surprise, a number of people expressed their enjoyment of these posts. Now after several years of writing the new Trogo, I have decided to collect some of them together, along with some of the older Trogo writings, and put them into a book—which you now hold in your hand.

I hope you enjoy these writings of mine. Yet, more importantly I hope they provoke you to think. And most importantly of all, I hope they serve the Lord's church through the promotion of a Christian worldview. In all that I do—teaching, preaching and writing—the overarching concern of my heart is the deterioration (or even loss) of a biblical view of life, morals and faith. In just my lifetime we have declined so much in this country, and in the West in general. We have become a largely post-Christian culture. This is not only true in society at large, but in the church as well. It is to combat this paradigm that I write and teach. So for those readers who hold to a Christian worldview, may these writings strengthen and encourage you in the faith. For anyone who does not view life from a biblical orientation, I pray that you will see the reasonableness and validity of Christianity and be brought to a knowledge of the truth. For me, truth is what it is all about. Remember, "grace and truth came through Jesus Christ" (John 1:17).

Victor Morris
August 2016

P.S. I purposely designed this collection of writings to be serious in tone. Perhaps later I will put together some of the more humorous pieces. You will have to wait until then to read "Thoughts on White Stuff." Sorry. V.

Essay 1
Spiritual Illiteracy

Sometimes I write just because I have to. Gotta get it out of my system. Chances are, I have seen something that peeves me, irritates me, or just plain ticks me off. Thus it is with this piece. So hold on, I'm about to vent.

I am often amazed how illiterate we are as a people. We have gotten to the place in America where it seems we almost prize ignorance and stupidity. We make heroes out of the Forrest Gumps of life. We wallow in the mindless, puerile (and often immoral) trash that is promoted as reality TV. We seem to prize ignorance and eschew knowledge. Our national educational test scores only retain any type of respectability because we continually lower the standards and reform the scoring systems. We devalue education, and in place of our own mores and values we let the government tells us what is right and wrong. And all the while our country sinks further into its self-imposed ignorant "bliss."

Let me give you an example. A recent article in *Reader's Digest* concerned the outrageous ignorance of many Americans. For example, studies show that most Americans can readily identify who Larry, Curley and Moe are, but they cannot identify the three branches of the Federal government. Also, people can name at least four or five of the seven dwarfs, but they are clueless when asked to name two justices of the Supreme Court. Good grief! Is it really that bad in our country? I am afraid the answer must be in the affirmative.

And sad to say, in the church we are no better than the rest of the society. One of the traditional roles of the church has been to foster and promote education, literacy and academics. Historically the church taught people to read so that the Word of God could be understood. The church founded institutions of higher education so servants of the Scriptures could be trained for ministry. The church established schools because it was believed that people created in God's image with a free will had a right to knowledge and self-determination.

Yet, where are we now? We are basically theologically illiterate and spiritually stupid. We accept popular doctrinal drivel without question. We hardly ever "try" the spirits to see if they be of God (1 John 4:1). We shun "judging prophets" (1 Corinthians 14:29). We allow our values and ideas and ideals to be handed to us via TV preachers who don't know a lexicon from a lamppost. We believe whatever we are told from the pulpit or the radio or the CD because we are too lazy to study for ourselves. How many Christian adults don't even know what a concordance is, much less how to use one? Mention Irenaeus, Tertullian, Chrysostom, Athanasius, Zwingli, Melanchthon, Bunyan, Jonathan Edwards, Whitefield, Finney, or Tozer... and most people look at you like you're speaking Martian. (Of course, they probably could name at least five of the seven dwarves!) How many Christians look neat and respectable and "holy" on the outside, but in their minds and hearts they are woefully and tragically ignorant of the basic teachings of the faith, how to witness, or what reasons to give for why Christianity should be believed? Our pews are filled with sanctified ignoramuses!

Let me give you two examples of what I am talking about. I remember once teaching a class when the subject of the *imago Dei*, the image of God, was raised. I was somewhat taken aback by how many in the class had the concept that the image of God was essentially a physical reality. "Oh, God must have a body—Adam was made in His image." "If we knew what Adam looked like, then we would know what God looked like." "Well, we know that God has eyes, and hands, and a backside—the Bible says so." Mercy, mercy! I felt like I had been teleported from the east coast and plopped down right in the middle of a Mormon Sunday School class in Provo!

Now on the surface, this may seem like innocent ignorance. (Yeah right! Sort of like the kind of innocence a toddler displays when he swallows a whole bottle of pills because he thinks it is candy.) Indeed, I can understand the tendency to interpret biblical anthropomorphisms too literally. Many have done so. But there is a more heinous doctrinal crime here. There is a basic flaw in this theology itself, that is, in the underlying concept of who God is. Think about it. When we make statements like those quoted in the previous paragraph, what are we really doing? Are we not defining God by looking at man? Our theology is anthropocentric, that is, man-centered. And man-centered theology is pagan and humanistic, not biblical or Christian.

Ponder this for a moment. I have over the years had to deal with this very same discussion repeatedly. We read that God created man in His own image. And what do we do? We usually begin by looking at human nature and from that we try to figure out what God is like.

Instead, shouldn't we look at God and try to figure out what characteristics that are similar to the Deity we find in humankind? Shouldn't our starting point be the Deity, not Adam? If God IS SPIRIT (John 4:24) then we know that the *imago Dei* must be a spiritual image, not physical. We must look to man's intellect, will, capacity to have relationship, emotions, the desire to respond in worship, and similar human traits as our focus for understanding the image of God. We must begin with who God is, and then see Him reflected in man, if we are to understand this concept. Not the reverse. If we define the image of God as physical, and we try to make Adam a corporeal clone of God (shades of Brigham Young and the Adam-god teaching!) then we have limited the very nature of God Himself. The Almighty is, well, not All-Mighty any more. In our minds He has become a being bound by flesh and limited by the laws of the physical space-time continuum. Heaven and all good sense forbid it!

Let me give you another example. I recently heard a sermon in which the subject of sin and holiness were being presented. The statement was made that God decides what is right based on what is good for His children. Sin, the reverse, is what harms men. God decides that something is wrong, and designates it as sin, because it hurts those He loves. You know what this teaching amounts to? Let me give it to in Latin: *Soapus Porcus*, i.e, HOGWASH.

Listen to me. You need to understand this. God doesn't arbitrarily choose what is right and what is wrong. He doesn't consult within the Holy Trinity and decide what is holy and what is sin. And He certainly doesn't use man's welfare as a measuring guide. There is no guide, no moral law, no standard outside of God that the Deity looks to in declaring what is sinful or not.

Instead, the truth is that sin is something that violates the very nature of God Himself. Whatever God does, He does in accordance with His own Being, His own holy and righteous nature. He cannot act otherwise. What He does comes from Who He is! Holiness, goodness and rightness is as intrinsic to Him as are eternity, infinity and omnipotence. What is consistent with the holy nature of the Almighty is good and right. What contradicts the nature of God is evil and sinful.

Do you see the problem? Once again there was a misguided attempt to understand spiritual truth from a man-centered perspective. Now, I agree that what is holy and good will produce benefit for human beings. And I also adamantly insist that what is sinful and wrong will bring ill results to people. But the effects of both of these things on people is not what determines what is right or wrong. Holiness is rooted in the Person of Yahweh. God declares most emphatically in His revealed Word, "Be holy, because I am holy." He did not say "Be holy because it will benefit you." No. Our holiness must be rooted in an emulation of the personal character of the Divine.

Guess what? As I listened to this sermon, I saw many heads nodding in agreement with this point. I thought to myself, here is a subtle form of humanistic heresy being accepted and affirmed by an entire congregation of Christians. God help us. No wonder Paul admonished, nay, commanded the Corinthians to judge (that is, discern, reasonably analyze, and critique) the proclaimed word of God. Humans are prone to error. We all err—myself most certainly included. The only adequate judge is the Holy Scriptures. But in order for that trustworthy standard to be enforceable we need Christian believers who are mature in understanding the Word and capable of using it effectively.

I will close with a challenge. One of the most skilled and best known preachers of the past century or so was a guy named G. Campbell Morgan. Morgan's commentaries and biblical expositions are still highly merited classics. In his day, Morgan was known as a Bible teacher and preacher extraordinaire. How did he get to be this way? By reading and studying the Bible with commitment and consistency. Yet, as capable, learned and well-studied as he was, he still knew that anytime he wrote or spoke on the Scriptures, he needed to further immerse himself in fresh study. Consequently, if he was preparing to preach on a particular book of the Bible, or write a study of it, he would read that book 40 to 50 times! Imagine that. What an example to us. What a challenge. How many of us don't even read the Word at all! God forgive us!

What is the result of our spiritual laziness and apathy? Dead churches. Lost people. An immoral culture. An ignorant church body. Lifeless and listless saints. Unchanged lives and worldly lifestyles. A nation which desperately needs spiritual renewal and yet remains without revival.

We are blind sheep following blind shepherds, and one day we will all fall into the ditch.

Essay 2
Sizing Up Greatness

When I was a kid I was fascinated by space and stars and the planets. I was a *Star Trek* geek before there were Trekkies. No matter how much fun I was having playing outside in the summer time, I would always come in to see what was happening that week with Kirk, Spock and Bones. Yes, I must confess, I was also an avid fan of *Lost in Space*. ("Danger! Danger! Be careful, Will Robinson!") I read Tom Swift and Danny Dunn. I loved movies like *Forbidden Planet, Earth Vs. The Flying Saucers* and *The Day The Earth Stood Still*. I was a space nut.

Indeed, my ambition as a youngster was to become an astronomer. (God had other plans.) And so with this fascination with astronomy, it is not surprising that many of my youthful science projects involved models of the solar system. I made more than my fair share of planets out of Play-Doh and Stryofoam balls. I was the king of coat hangers and clay spheres. Yet, with all my juvenile enthusiasm I still missed something. I failed to comprehend the vastness of space. In fact, as is probably common with most young astronomers, I thought my wire and Stryofoam creations were pretty realistic.

This all changed for me a few years back. I was working on a series of classes on basic theology that I called "God 101." We were studying the essential attributes of God. You know, His omniscience, infinity, eternity, immutability... that sort of stuff. When we came to the week where we were to study God's omnipresence, I decided to use the size of the solar system as a model. I wanted to illustrate the vastness of space, and then make the point that God is present throughout all the created order. I also wanted to emphasize that as immense as space is, and God governs and oversees all that goes on in the entire universe, He still has time and interest in each of us. To prepare for this lesson I went to the internet to find a good way of conveying the size of the solar system. I found several models—all of which surprised me. They showed me that my own understanding of the magnitude of the solar system's size was limited indeed. Let me share with you the model that I used...

Imagine that the earth itself were the size of a peppercorn, you know those small black things that chef Emeril insists must be ground fresh on every dish in his kitchen. Anyway, the earth is a peppercorn. On this scale one inch is equal to 100,000 miles, and the sun is the size of a basketball. Get the idea? Now based on this scheme, how far away would the earth be from the sun? In reality the earth is 93 million miles from the sun. In our model the peppercorn earth is 78 feet away from the basketball sun. (Try it. Take a basketball and get about 80 feet away. You will find that the basketball looks about the same size as the sun does in the sky.) Let's try some other measurements. If the earth is a peppercorn, then Mercury is a pinhead, Saturn is a hazelnut, and the mighty planet Jupiter is just a pecan. How about

Essay 2: *Sizing Up Greatness*

distance? Mercury is 30 feet from the sun. Jupiter is 405 feet out from the sun. And the most distance planet, Pluto? Well it's the size of a pin point and it's 3057 feet from the sun, over *half a mile away*. Yep, half a mile! Think that's amazing, it gets better. The closest star to us is Promixa Centauri, which is 4.2 light years away from earth. In our scale model that would be 4200 miles away. (Keep in mind, the entire earth is only the size of a peppercorn.) Want to go farther? Well, the center of our Milky Way Galaxy is a mere 26,000,000 miles away from us. Now understand, this is not 26 million miles in reality, this is 26 million miles on our earth-is-a-peppercorn scale. On this scale, our galaxy has a diameter of about 100,000,000 miles. Yes, on this basketball-sun scale, the Milky Way is 100 million miles across!

Furthermore, it must be remembered that as huge as our own solar system seems to us, that our sun is only one of billions of stars scattered throughout the Milky Way Galaxy. And there are other suns and star systems vastly larger than our own. And then we must remind ourselves that our own galaxy is only one among the billions and billions of galaxies that are scattered throughout the known universe. It truly boggles the mind. It is beyond our ability to comprehend in any meaningful way. We can speak of the numbers, but I think it is overwhelming to us to try to really grab hold of the concept of the immensity of space. We really cannot conceive of the size of the universe.

Now to my main point… such information is currently often used to denigrate the philosophers, scientists and (especially) theologians of the ancient past. For centuries, most notably in the church world, an anthropocentric view held sway in Western men's thinking. It was accepted as axiomatic that mankind was the center of the universe. Humanity was the highest and greatest creation of God, and mankind was the focus of the created order and of the Creator's attention. Such a view was easily validated by an earth-centered cosmology. But Copernicus, Galileo, and their cronies upset all this. They demonstrated that the sun, not the earth, is the center of our solar system. More modern scientists have shown us that the sun is not even the center of our galaxy. Sol wings it way through the heavens almost on the fringes of the Milky Way. Mankind does not seem to be at the center of ANYTHING.

Thus as our knowledge of the universe expands, our regard for puny little homo sapiens diminishes. This has led to a popular perspective today, i.e, that mankind is indeed small and insignificant when compared with the entire cosmos. This means that man is really not all that important. We humans are only arrogant and presumptuous if we assume that in the greatness of this cosmic reality we are really anything important at all. Surely if there is a God, He would not create all this huge universe for such a lowly, insignificant thing as humanity.

Many interesting and disturbing concepts arise from this perspective. For example, this view asserts that man's existence is only an incidental occurrence in the hugeness of the natural reality. He has no intrinsic meaning or purpose. There is no design or pattern to the cosmos—for surely the Divine would not be so foolish as to create this gigantic universe to serve one species on one smallish planet. Probably there are millions, nay, billions of other worlds with intelligent species on them. It only makes sense. There has to be SOMEBODY else out there in all that space! Some would even go so far as to say that the enormous scope of the universe argues against the existence of God. How could a Deity with any kind of wisdom or intelligence create something so immense, and so meaningless, for one tiny world and one scrawny species?

The question may be asked, no, demands to be asked: What is man in the vastness of this universe? Who are the children of men that they should be considered of any worth or importance? (Do these questions sound familiar?) In the immensity of space, where does man fit in? Let's attempt an answer.

First of all, the point has to be made that the question itself is all wrong. The basic idea that size determines value is false to begin with. I think of my wife. Sue is about 5 foot 3 inches tall.

I love her with all my heart. She is the dearest and most precious person in all the world to me. But you know what, I would not love her less if she suddenly shrank to 4' 11". And I would not love her more if she suddenly grew to be six feet tall. Her worth is not dependent on her size. Her value in my eyes is not a consequence of how tall or short she is. Indeed, there are many things in this world that are huge compared with her. Mount Everest is gargantuan. But I love Sue more than Mt. Everest. The Pacific Ocean is vast, but my wife is more important to me than that ocean.

Of course, you say, but here we are only talking about relatively small changes in size. What is the difference between 5 feet and 5 miles compared to the size of the universe? But don't you see, it all only a matter of degree. If my valuing of a person would not change if they grew 9 inches, neither would it change if a person (or thing) were 10 trillion times bigger. (And I must say if I had to choose between Sue and the Andromeda Galaxy, I would choose Sue.)

I think God views things in much the same way. Love and relationship are what God is all about. It is the essence of who He is. (After all, He existed in eternal Trinitarian fellowship before the worlds began.) God's yardstick of value is not based on physical size, but on the intrinsic value with which He created each thing. And mankind was created in His image. The stars were not. Planets were not made to reflect His personhood. Solar systems were not made to have relationship with Him. Nebulae do not have souls. Jesus did not die for galaxies.

Remember I hinted that the questions we were addressing had a familiar ring to them. They should. David asked the very same questions 3000 years ago. "What is man, that You are mindful of him? And the son of man, that You visit him?" (Psalm 8:4). Do you remember David's answer? "You have made him a little lower than the angels." Amazing. And actually, even more amazing in the original Hebrew. David literally says, "You have made him [man] a little lower than _Elohim_." Elohim is the most common name for God in the Hebrew Bible. God, in making mankind in His own image, made him a little lower than God! Now understand me, I have not converted to Mormonism. I understand that God is infinite, and so far above us that we cannot conceive it. But, as much as it is possible for finite, created, fleshly humanity to be like the infinite, uncreated, Spirit of the Creator, so we are. Wonderful!

This means we have great value in God's eyes. And even in our fallenness, we have the remnants of the original glory of our creation. As has been said, "Man may be fallen, but he is not junk." There is worth in the human creature because God created us, and He created us in His image with purpose, design, dignity and value. How much value? Well, enough that God would send His Son to die to redeem us from our fallen state.

So God does not consider the physical size of something to determine its importance. He values a thing, or a person, based on the nature of its creation. Yes, man is the center of the universe and the focus of creation. This is true because of God, His plan and purpose for us, and His sovereign choice in creating us as He did. Our worth is derived directly from the Creator.

Yet, a question may still be lurking in the back of your mind: Why then would God create such an immensely huge universe? I don't know. I must leave that to the Mind who made it all. However, I can speculate on a few possible reasons. (These satisfy *my* mind, at least.)

Essay 2: *Sizing Up Greatness*

1) God often conveys truth to us in imagery. Think of the Passover sacrificial lamb, Christ as the Rock, God riding the storm clouds, Abraham sacrificing Isaac, God sitting on a throne... all of these are examples. How then could God display to us His immensity, His omnipresence, His glory? Perhaps the universe itself is one huge object lesson on the greatness of God.

2) God sees and knows all. I do not know what exists on some planet revolving some star circling around the center of the Andromeda Galaxy. But God knows. And perhaps He created some thing of tremendous beauty on that planet that simply exists to give HIM pleasure. Who knows, perhaps there are trillions and trillions of such things out there whose entire purpose for existing is to glorify and please God (see Revelation 4:11). I don't even need to know about these things, for He knows. And that is sufficient.

3) God is the infinite and eternal Optimist. He created the world, the Garden of Eden, and even the Tree of Life, with the purpose of providing for unfallen humanity. He did this even though He knew that we would actually fall. We cannot understand what might have been had Adam and Eve not fallen. Imagine six thousand years of perfect human existence. No sin. No disease. No death. No war or crime. Virtually no limits to human creativity, exploration or scientific endeavor. If we had not sinned, might we not have been out amongst those stars and galaxies by now. Perhaps God created this huge universe in anticipation of it being occupied by His children. And we blew it.

4) In the ages to come, God will create new heavens, and a new earth. But consider... He will create new HEAVENS. It

seems that the new heavens will be much like our present universe, although pure, uncorrupted and untainted by sin. Could it be that in the eternal eras to come, we will indeed be occupying those planets and galaxies scattered throughout this universe?

One final thought regarding this matter of size and importance. If any would still assert that we should consider something important based on its size—then how do you explain the Incarnation? When God the Son, infinite and immortal Deity, came to earth, how did He come? He came not as a giant. He did not come as a great king. He was not even an adult. He came as a frail, small, helpless baby. Eternity clothed in the minutes of measured time. Infinity wrapped in swaddling clothes. Omnipotence finding life-giving nourishment at His mother's breast. God, the Almighty, lying in a manger. Little. Weak. Seemingly insignificant. But as C. S. Lewis said in *The Last Battle*, "Once in our world, a Stable had something in it that was bigger than our whole world."

Essay 3
Forgive Me, O Great Gaia!

Okay, so here is my beef. If you are going to believe in evolution, then be consistent about it. Don't say you believe in the evolution of species—which generally presupposes God as either nonexistent or irrelevant, and blind chance as the motivating force of reality—and then use theistic and creationist terminology.

What am I talking about? Well, some time back I saw one of those nature programs on *PBS*. Now I like *PBS*. I find many of its programs interesting and informative. But I have to take their worldview with a grain of salt. (Should I say "lump"? How about enough salt to make soup in Lake Superior?) Their programs that deal with nature and science always have an evolutionary bias. I have come to expect it, and can usually choose to ignore it. ("Liar!" I get somewhat upset every time.)

But this one program sticks in my mind, and I can't just forget it. I am watching this program on birds and wetlands. In case you don't know, I am somewhat of a birder, so I am really enjoying this program. I watch various beautiful scenes of birds, wetlands, prairies and mountain vistas. Well, suddenly this nice nature walk turns into a lecture on conservation. No problem—except that in the middle of this treatise on environmentalism, evolution and the competition of species gets thrown in. Then we start hearing about "man's role," "mankind's responsibility," and our "stewardship of the earth."

Hello! Does anybody out there understand the concept of stewardship and responsibility? Stewardship means you are holding something in trust for someone else. Responsibility means we will answer to someone else for our actions. If we are stewards of the earth, to whom are we responsible? Doesn't saying we are stewards of the earth assume that there is someone (some One?) to whom we will answer for how we treat this earth?

By the way, while we are talking about this stuff—there was another thought that occurred to me while watching this program. As is typical with such *PBS* fare, humanity got the rap as being the bad egg in the universe's Easter basket. I guess you could say, we are the thorn in Gaia's side.

But let us assume for a minute that the philosophical bias of this *PBS* program is true—that we all arrived here on the evolutionary highway. Isn't evolution essentially amoral and ethically neutral? If evolution is true, there is no good or bad involved—just what is, i.e., what has evolved. No one faults foxes for eating rabbits, or lady bugs for eating aphids. So why does mankind, only an evolved primate, become the pimple on evolution's face? (A face that had its cosmetics applied randomly, I might add.)

Essay 3: *Forgive Me, O Great Gaia!*

It seems to me that if man has developed the intelligence to learn how to exploit the environment, to rape the land, to wantonly kill and destroy animal and plant species—well, who is to complain? (And to whom?) Evolution, along with the chaotic blind goddess Chance, has brought homo sapiens to this point. We are the top competitors in the field, the masters of natural selection. So what if we kill off spotted owls or dodo birds or Bengal tigers... we have evolved to the point of being able to do so. Who is to say we are wrong? Who's to say there is such a thing as wrong?

Unless...

Unless, evolution is a bunch of bunk, and random acts of nature did not bring us to this point... Unless creation is a fact, and there is a Moral Agent who started the whole shebang going... Unless there is a Creator, and HE did make us, and we are going to answer to HIM one day!

Then you do have stewardship. And responsibility. And moral choices. And right and wrong—including how we treat the environment!

You can't have your cake (of moral responsibility) and eat it too (i.e., have it devoured by blind, random chance).

Sorry, Darwin.

Essay 4
What Evil Lurks in the Hearts of Men

I am thinking this afternoon about the nature of evil. Possibly a rather strange subject to be contemplating on a Friday afternoon. Maybe it's all the bizarre crimes that we hear about these days. Or maybe it's the violence raging its way through the Middle East right now. Or perhaps it's simply the clouds and gloom that I see outside my office window. Whatever the reason, the matter of evil keeps coming to mind.

Evil is one of those realities of life that we all live with, suffer through, and accept (to a certain degree). We grudgingly recognize it as a normal part of life. We concede its influence and inevitability, though with reluctance. We all know that at times our only recourse is to choose "the lesser of two evils," as much as we hate to admit the necessity of such a regrettable decision. We long for a perfect world—dreaming of utopia—yet all the while living next door to hell. We shake our heads in disbelief at the latest brutality reported on the evening news—as though this was the first time we had ever known of such a thing, choosing to forget that we heard much the same kind of news last week. There is a certain element of denial, it seems, in living with evil. Reading the latest rape statistics or watching a special news report on domestic violence elicits the same kind of response we feel at the death of a loved one—we don't believe it at first because we really don't want to believe it at all. Evil, like death, is something that we weren't originally created to experience. And so our inner frame, the internal make-up of our being, shudders in disbelief when exposed to it.

I think that part of our incredulous reaction to evil's presence may be the result of the nature of evil itself. So let us consider this question. What is evil? What exactly is its nature? How does it function and what causes it to happen? Specifically, does evil have its own being, its own reality—or is it the lack of some reality?

At first glance, the answer may seem simple. Something as pervasively influential, ubiquitous and persistent as evil must exist in its own right. Look around. The world is full of evil. There are natural evils: hurricanes, floods, tornadoes, fires, lightning strikes, and earthquakes abounding. And there are no fewer moral evils to deal with: murder, rape, theft, lying, infidelity, abuse, violence, racism, blasphemy, idolatry, greed… and the list could go on until we are sick of it. Evil exists, plainly, obviously so.

But I press the point. Does evil "exist"? I challenge you to think of about this, to really ponder it. Does evil really exist? Or could it be that that what we perceive as the reality of evil is actually the non-existence of something, the lack of a certain reality.

Essay 4: *What Evil Lurks in the Hearts of Men*

Let me use an analogy to explain what I mean. Suppose a man were very ill. Some dread disease has ravished his body for months on end. He now finds himself weak to an extreme degree. He can barely lift his arms to feed himself. It is an effort to raise his own body to sit on the edge of the bed. Now is that man's weakness a thing in itself, or is his weakness actually the lack of something—muscular strength and ability? Is weakness an active force that is working on his physical body, or is it the lack of physical capacity that makes him what we call "weak." Is weakness actually a thing in itself, or it is rather the lack of a particular thing that is usually present? Is not the answer obvious? Weakness is not a force, power or activity in and of itself. Instead, weakness is the lack of something—strength.

May I now apply the analogy to our larger discussion? Is evil a force or action in itself? I do not think so. In fact, that is to credit evil with too much. It is to give evil an essential reality that it cannot have. In a sense, to view evil as a thing in itself would be to assert it as being a positive factor or force. How absurd! For evil is only a negative.

Allow me to use some moral illustrations to further illuminate the topic. Take cowardice for example. Should we consider cowardice as an active influence in a person's life? Or does it not make more sense to view cowardice as the lack of courage? Is fear something that acts in a positive way on a person's mind and heart? Or is it rather the absence of confidence, faith or trust? Get the idea? Now for a classic example. What about hate? Do we really want to endow hatred with an active, positive capability? Is hate a thing in itself? Or would it be better to consider hatred as what is left in a person's heart when love, kindness, compassion or goodwill is missing?

These examples are rather easy to see, I think. Some others may be a little more difficult to conceptualize. Take sexual lust, for example. If anything appears to be a driving, forceful actuality it would seem to be lust. But is it? The sex drive is a normal, positive compelling dynamic in a human being. But when there is a lack of moral restraint and the absence of purity and holiness in a person's heart, then lust results. Lust itself is simply a natural, wholesome, positive quality that has gone awry. How about greed? This may seem to be a rather direct urge in a person's life. But if we go deeper, is greed a thing in itself? Or might we discover that a greedy person is actually one who lacks trust in God's provision, or deserts love of spiritual matters for the love of material things, or lacks a proper understanding of what is truly valuable in life? There may be many different causes of the evil, and it may vary its manifestation from person to person. However, the essential nature of greed itself demonstrates that it is a negative, not a positive quality of the human heart.

Is there biblical warrant for such a view of evil? Yes, indeed. For instance, there are several words in the Hebrew Bible that are translated "sin." One of these is awen. This word carries the idea of something that is weak or worthless. It seems to be related to the Hebrew word for "nothingness" (*ayin*). It connotes the deficiency of true worth. Thus, sin is presented as the lack of something. We also see this negative quality in the most common word for sin in Greek, which is *hamartia*. This word literally means to "miss the mark." Sin is to be off center, to miss the target, to not be where we should be. Again, the idea of deficiency or lack is evident. Thus, we see that even in Scripture we have the idea that evil is a want of goodness, it is missing something—not the presence of something.

Based on all this, we now understand that moral evil is not a positive reality at all. Instead, it is a deficiency of rightness, of virtue, of what is good. It is the lack of those qualities or tendencies that actively work to make us godly, that motivates us to be what we were created to be—good, virtuous and righteous.

Essay 4: *What Evil Lurks in the Hearts of Men*

Okay, you say, this is an interesting discussion (at least I hope you find it to be so) but what does this have to do with my life on this dreary Friday afternoon? I tell you what... tons! We need this understanding so much. I think that one of the most devilish deceptions that most people face is the belief that they can "pull themselves up by their own bootstraps," that they can just "turn over a new leaf" whenever they want. Satan, the ultimate deficient one, the one with huge amounts of emptiness and lack in his spiritual reality, deceives us into believing that we can do something regarding the terrible plight we are in as human beings. (Even Christians fall prey to this lie.) What folly!

The problem with human nature is that we are flawed and fallen. We have lost our spiritual link to God, and thus we are lost in life's journey. The biggest need in our lives is the void in our souls, our lack of spiritual excellence (virtue). We are born sinners—which means we lack essential goodness and moral strength. We are all prone to do wrong, because we do not have the wherewithal to do right. (In theology this is called depravity.) The only goodness and moral rightness we find in the human race is the positive influence of God's truth, God's Spirit, and God's people (more on them in a moment). If there is virtue in the human race it is the direct result of the common grace of a good and merciful God. We can't help ourselves otherwise. We are incapable of changing our degenerate, deficient hearts. Asking a fallen, sinful human being to be virtuous is like asking an armless man to arm wrestle. He just doesn't have the necessary equipage to do it.

Now, understand me—I don't denigrate and devalue mankind because of this. Rather, I agree with Francis Schaeffer when he said, "Man may be sinful, but he is not junk." How true! If anyone would question the value of man, he would only need to look at the Cross to find himself corrected. Mankind was valuable enough to God that the cost for our redemption was the life of the Deity Himself! What greater evidence could we desire before we could accept the worth of every person in the sight of God?

But, and here's the rub, there is still the problem of sin, of evil. Every one of us needs to be filled with those qualities and essential traits that we all lack. We are all deficient in a very fundamental way. (In a real way, before coming to Christ we are "sub-human," less than human beings were designed to be. In Christ, we are raised to again enjoy the true humanity that Adam once knew in his primitive state. But we boast not of this raised status, for it is all by grace!) Without Christ, we are all empty, needy, deficient creatures, awaiting the filling of His goodness. How rightly did Pascal say in the *Pensées* that there is an emptiness in man that "he tries in vain to fill with everything around him… [but] this infinite abyss can be filled only with an infinite and immutable object; in other words by God." And as much as nature abhors a vacuum, God does so even more. He longs to fill our evil, empty hearts with His loving, righteous fullness.

And wonder of wonders—He graciously does so. How many millions can testify to this fact! As a result, we who were as empty and lacking as any other sinful person, find our lack taken care of by His goodness. Our deficiency is overwhelmed by His sufficiency.

And after this individual transformation and infilling of virtue, we then find that He calls on us to be part of the solution for the evil of this world. We learn that we can be a positive force to counteract the deficiencies so prevalent around us. We find that by acting in cooperation with the Holy Spirit that we can actually combat the emptiness of evil with the abundance of God's grace. And for ourselves personally, we discover that in Him we are more than adequately equipped to deal with whatever comes our way in life—that we are sufficiently enabled to confidently face life with power, virtue, joy and peace.

Child of God, are you like I am? Are there some days when you feel overwhelmed with your own sense of inadequacy and insufficiency? Take hope. Have confidence. He who is the fullness of life, the all in all, the rich Source for everyone who has need—He has promised to deliver us from this dreary and struggling existence and to supply all our lack with His abundant provision. What a wonderful promise and joyous prospect!

(See 2 Corinthians 3:4-5, Romans 7:18-8:2, Colossians 1:12-13)

Essay 5
Is Jesus the Only Way?

Just recently one of our ministry partners at Advancing Native Missions, a brother from East Africa, visited the seminary of a major Evangelical denomination. He spoke to a group of graduate students in a class on missiology. You would think that such a group of missiological students would be pretty well grounded in a biblical worldview, especially when it comes to evangelism, missions and a Christian understanding of salvation. You would think…

Our indigenous missionary friend asked these students a few questions. He wanted to test the waters. One question was this: If a person is not a Christian, and has not heard the Gospel, will he be eternally doomed to hell? Simple question. And from a biblical understanding of things... a simple answer. But in this situation—not so! A minority of the students immediately answered in the affirmative. A minority! Another minority answered with a resounding "NO," that person would not go to hell. Most of the students were not sure. There ensued a discussion/debate as to the fate of those dying without the Gospel.

I was shocked and disheartened to hear this report. What has happened to us? How far has the church fallen from its heritage? How bankrupt have we become? Have we really wandered that far from a Christian paradigm... a biblical understanding of truth?

Sad to say, the answer is "Yes!"

Need I recount the clear biblical teaching on this subject? For the Bible is clear:

- Jesus is THE Way to the Father, and no one comes to the Father but through Him—John 14:6

- There is salvation in NO other name than that of Jesus—Acts 4:12

- He who does not have the Son of God DOES NOT have life—1 John 5:12

- He who believes in Jesus has life; He who does not believe in Jesus SHALL NOT see life—John 3:36

- And, He that does not believe the Gospel "shall be DAMNED!"—Mark 16:16

So the Bible is plain. The biblical view is evident. Indeed, this very issue is dealt with great perception and insight by Paul in Romans 1:16-25.

Essay 5: *Is Jesus the ONLY WAY?*

Yet this very simple understanding of biblical truth was not within the thinking of these students. This raises a lot of questions. Indeed, there are several very serious issues here.

1. The matter of missions and evangelism itself is the first issue. If people without Christ are not lost, why the mandate from Christ to go preach the Gospel? Missions is only necessary, if people are lost without Christ. Did Jesus send us on a millennia-long wild goose chase just for the fun of it? If so, explain that to the martyrs who have given, and even today are giving their lives for the sake of the Gospel!

2. The integrity of Christ Himself comes into question. It was Jesus who claimed to be the ONLY way to the Father. It was Jesus who mandated world evangelization. It was Jesus who sent out His witnesses/martyrs for the proclamation of the Gospel. It was Jesus who declared that anyone who does not believe is condemned eternally. Was He mistaken? Did Jesus lie to us… or was He just ignorant of the truth? Was He ignorant of the real situation? Did He only think He was THE Way? The very Person of the Savior Himself becomes suspect here.

3. The trustworthiness of the Bible becomes dubious. It is the Bible, in the passages above and many others like them, which proclaims the doctrine of the lostness of mankind without the Savior. If the Bible is not true, not doctrinally dependable in this matter, what about its other teachings? Are men lost at all? Is the Fall real? Do we need the Savior? Is Jesus really the Savior? The truth of who God is becomes doubtful. The reality of who Christ is—His true deity, His very humanity, His dual nature, His sinless perfection, the atoning work, the bodily resurrection, His authority and

power—all is based on a historical faith grounded in the revealed Word of God. Toss out the doctrine of Christ as (necessary) Savior and everything else is up for grabs!

Do you see what is happening here? This is but another example of how things are shifting in the church. Our worldview is changing. A thoroughly Christian worldview is slipping away from the Body of Christ, and we are sliding into… what? Humanism? Existentialism? Postmodernism? Naturalism? Something else? It really doesn't matter. Each of these is a dead end. No, let me take that back. The sliding away from a Christian and biblical worldview is not a dead end. It has a very precise, well-defined end. It is called heresy, a broad path that leads to destruction—in other words, hell. And no debate can change that.

"Let God be true, but every man a liar" (Romans 3:4).

Essay 6
The Descent of Man

By now, you would think I should quit being surprised. Yet, I still find myself constantly being amazed at people's abject ignorance. Far too many people are just plain gullible, accepting whatever nonsense comes down the pike. If a little knowledge is a dangerous thing, then a little misinformation coupled with tons of ignorance must have the same potential as a hydrogen bomb!

Let me tell you what started all this personal shock and ire. I was reading something I had written a few years ago. It concerned a revealing conversation that Sue, my darling bride, became involved in. Revealing in the sense that the conversation exposed people's innate capacity to believe foolishness. My wife's field of expertise is education, especially the education of those with learning problems. She has spent many years studying and teaching children (and adults) who have learning disabilities. She knows her stuff. So she was intrigued, and a little frustrated, to become involved in a group conversation that dealt with the subject of dyslexia. One person present was pontificating on a theory that attempts to explain away dyslexia in terms of social evolution. This theory holds that one category of people learns one way, and another category learns completely differently, based on whether they are hunter-gatherers or farmers by nature. Dyslexics, according to this theory, are hunter-gatherers. And, of course, the poor, misunderstood hunter-gatherers are castigated and denigrated by the more numerous and socially acceptable farmer learners. Alas, poor hunter-gatherers! How preposterous! Sue was appropriately irritated by this folderol.

When Sue was discussing this theory with me, I was equally irritated—not only by this idiotic concept posing as educational theory, but also by the unstated but assumed underlying social theory. What do I mean? Simply this—what we have here is the common presupposition that all humanity has undergone a certain specific type of social evolution. This social theory applies Darwinistic principles to our understanding of anthropology and asserts that our cultural evolution went something like this...

- We began as brute beasts who gathered berries and roots for survival, just a step above chimps and baboons.

- Gradually we worked our way up to hunting (I guess fishing too, for all you anglers out there).

- Then finally we developed rudimentary agricultural skills, eventually becoming... (Tah-dah!) farmers. Yea!

Thus, it is posited, just as we see the organic evolution of species in all of nature, so in the course of history we have seen the social evolution of human patterns, functions and skills.

My estimation of Darwinian social theory? In a word: HOGWASH!

If we are to believe the Bible as historically accurate, then we must reject this theory without hesitation. Let's go back to the beginning. In Genesis 2:15 we see Adam in the Garden of Eden. He is given instruction by God to "dress and keep" the garden (or "work it and take care of it" as the NIV renders it). In the curse that God placed on Adam after the Fall, God specifically mentions man's painful toil in working the ground (see Genesis 3:17-19). When Cain and Abel brought their offerings to the Lord, Cain brought fruits and vegetables, while Abel brought a sacrifice from his flocks (Genesis 4:2-4). All these passages indicate that farming and raising livestock both were practiced by the earliest human beings. Agriculture was not something that developed over many millennia of human progress. It has been a common feature of human society since the beginning (see also Genesis 4:20).

While we are in Genesis, note that the biblical account of man's early history records another interesting fact. This is that the building of cities came soon after the Fall (see Genesis 4:17). Civilization was not a late development that only occurred after hundreds of generations of organic and social evolution. Instead, the tendency for urbanization came very near the beginning of human history.

One other pertinent fact is worth noting. The commonly accepted social evolutionary theory asserts that men were first hunter-gatherers, and then developed agricultural skills. ("Ugh, deer and berries good!" came first. Only afterwards came: "Mmm! Dear, the biscuits and gravy were delicious!") But according to the Genesis record, man was not even allowed to hunt and kill animals for food until after the Flood (see Genesis 9:2-3). This was over 1000 years after the Creation.

The conclusion then is obvious. The secular anthropologists and humanistic sociologists are wrong—backward in fact. Mankind was first a farmer, and then a hunter.

But (I hear you ask it) what about all that anthropological evidence? How do we explain cave men, Neanderthal and Cro-Magnon man? Do we not even today see people in the jungles and the bush living very primitive lives? Just think of all those National Geographic magazines we looked at as kids. Remember those simple natives, wearing leaves and eating berries, hunting birds with bows or blow guns. Don't such tribal peoples prove that we came from primitive hunter-gatherer forebears? In fact, they do not. ("Oog! Me no understand.")

First of all, sometimes these tribal people are not as primitive as they seem. Anybody remember the Tasaday? They were supposed to be an aboriginal people in the Philippines who lived an extremely uncivilized and simple existence. After their discovery, anthropologists and social scientists flocked to the Philippines to investigate the primeval Tasaday. The only thing was—the Tasaday were not so uncivilized and simple as they appeared. It turned out the whole thing was a clever hoax. The Tasaday actually had to be coached in the fine art of being primitive.

Secondly, the existence of primitive tribes does not prove that this was the way mankind existed in previous eras. It simply means that there are such people on earth today. Period. But didn't they evolve from some half-ape, half-human ancestors? No. But didn't they get locked away by dense jungles in out-of-the-way locations, and then just live for millennia in their original, primeval status quo? I don't think so.

Rather, I think they are tribes that did indeed get isolated from the rest of humanity—and then degenerated to become what they are today. Looking at the matter from a biblical perspective, mankind is not the result of evolving from such flagrantly primitive states. Instead, we understand that the opposite is true. Mankind was at first civilized, and then fell into less sophisticated modes of living. If anything, we can say that because of the Fall mankind is not evolving but devolving. We are definitely not getting better, no matter what popular mythology says.

Bottom Line: Tribes who live in a hunter-gatherer existence are not proofs of social evolution, but rather of social entropy. They demonstrate the tendency of fallen man to degenerate. They are living witnesses of the "Descent of Man." Ugh!

Essay 7
Supermarkets, Sundays and Sanctity

I grew up in the suburbs of Richmond, Va. One fond memory is of a well-known Richmond institution—a family-owned chain of grocery stores called Ukrops. First opened in 1937, the stores were a regional phenomenon, known for quality products and attentive service. (You get a glimpse of their approach when you understand that their bag boys were known as "courtesy clerks" and they were required to take your groceries out to your car, regardless of the weather.) The Ukrops in-store delis were incredible. They became hot meeting places for people up and down the social scale. Indeed, their sandwiches were so good that many corporate executives would plan lunch meetings at the local Ukrops deli—power lunches in a grocery store! Can you imagine?

However, in my mind there was one overarching feature that stood out about the Ukrops stores: They exemplified Christian virtue. The Ukrops family were Christian people. And their Christian morals and principles carried over into how they ran their stores. The stores were clean, friendly and pleasant to be in. They did not sell alcoholic beverages. It was an annual tradition for the local newspapers to print a story about the grocery chain when the Sports Illustrated swimsuit was released—because Ukrops would not sell that particular issue. There were signs posted in their stores encouraging people to attend church. And get this, none of their stores were open on Sunday.

Yep. You did understand me correctly. Their stores were closed on Sundays. Now, I am not talking about a chain of stores operating in the 1930's. I am talking about a grocery chain that was in business until just a couple of years ago. (Ukrops was bought out by a national grocery chain in 2009.) Now you might expect that this caused them quite a bit of financial hardship. How can you close one day a week and compete with Safeway, Kroger, Martins, and other national chains? But actually for years Ukrops had the highest sales figures of any grocery chain in the Richmond area. This stat stood the test of time (and Sabbath closings) for quite a while.

There is a basic (and biblical) principle at work here. You honor God and He will honor you. Simple. Fact. Period.

You see, the Ukrops family took keeping the Sabbath day holy not merely as a suggestion, nor even as an Old Testament legalistic requirement. They considered it a sacred duty that honored God and observed His way of doing things. To them, Sunday was sacred. My, what a concept.

It is this focus on something actually being honored as holy—sacred, set apart—that fascinates me. Holiness is like a foreign language to many people—too many, in fact. They just don't seem to understand it. I see many Christians whose behavior, speech and values are not very different from those who do not know Christ. Indeed, there are far, far too many believers who exhibit lifestyles that are virtually indistinguishable from the way people in the world live. I fear we have truly lost something wonderful. We have lost a desire for holiness, and we have even lost a sense of the holy.

It is this sense of the holy that I think the church desperately needs to regain. But instead, we want to pretend that all things are holy (when they definitely are not!). It's sorta like when people want to treat all children exactly the same. Give awards to all participants in a contest. Reward alike any and all behaviors. Make no distinctions based on performance, achievement or merit. For after all, it is said, everyone is special. But this is simply not true. For someone to be "special" it requires that there to be something distinctive, noteworthy, or different about that person. If everyone is special, then no one is special. And it is also true for holiness. If everything is "holy" then nothing is really holy.

Let's refresh our minds about what holiness means. To be holy means to be set apart, distinct, other than, separate—indeed, special. It is not the usual, the ordinary. It is different. It is not your kitchenware—rather it is the holy tongs and utensils used to handle the fire of the altar, or the sacrifice on the altar. It is not your dining room table; it is the Table of the Presence, where the Bread of God is reserved for sacred use. It is not a Yankee candle in a jar; it is the Golden Altar where the smoke of the consecrated incense billows upward as a memorial before God. It is something spiritually special—something dedicated, devoted to God.

Our lives are to be like this. Holy. Separate. Different. Other than the world. We are called a "peculiar people" not because we are odd or strange, but rather because we are a different people. We are not of this world. We belong to another world, and another Being. We are

His, and we are to demonstrate what it really means to be His by how we live. We are to be holy. (See 1 Peter 1:16.)

Have you ever had a chance to read the diaries and journals of the great saints of times past? If not, let me encourage you to do so. There are great lessons and wise instruction for us in the pages of these heart-stirring works. I vividly remember reading the diary of David Brainerd many years ago. Brainerd was the son-in-law of noted pastor and theologian Jonathan Edwards. Brainerd was also a missionary to the American Indians. He spent his life for God, very literally. He basically used himself up for the sake of the Gospel. Here was a man of incredible devotion to God and inspiring dedication to the Lord's work. Yet, when you read his diary, you see how he wrestled with anguish over his own failings. He saw the lack in his own heart, and he longed for a life and a soul completely pure and holy before God. Listen to one excerpt from his diary...

"When I really enjoy God, I feel my desires of him the more insatiable, and my thirstings after holiness the more unquenchable.... Oh, for holiness! Oh, for more of God in my soul! Oh, this pleasing pain! It makes my soul press after God.... Oh, that I may feel this continual hunger, and not be retarded, but rather animated by every 'cluster from Cannan,' To reach forward in the narrow way, for the full enjoyment and possession of the heavenly inheritance."

I read such words, and I am struck to the core of my being. Do I have an insatiable, "continual hunger" for God? Is my thirst for holiness unquenchable? Do I even desire the "pleasing pain" of longing for true purity of soul? The truth is, I settle so often for so much less than this. My longings are too often more carnal than spiritual. My desires are for more of this world rather than having insatiable cravings for the One who made the world. My problem is not that I don't desire holiness, but I desire it too feebly.

Essay 7: *Supermarkets, Sundays and Sanctity*

Yet, there is some hope here also. Brainerd gives us a prescription we would be wise to follow. God, in His grace, blesses our lives with times of pleasure in His presence. When these experiences come, let's use them. Let the enjoyment of God induce in us that yearning for God and holiness we need. Let those blessed and joyous encounters with Him, those "clusters from Canaan," awake within us a hunger for more—more holiness in my own heart, more purity in my soul, more of Him in my life.

God, may we long for You, and to be holy in your sight!

Now, for a moment, let us return to the story of the Ukrops family and their stores. I think there is also a prescription for us here. Brainerd paints us a picture of someone pursuing holiness and the holy God. He tells us to "reach forward in the narrow way." But in a sinful world and godless culture, this pursuit of holiness must be very intentional. We have to decide on it, and then go after it with diligence. I think something that can help us in this regard is to recapture a sense of the holy in many areas of life. We need to ensure that our lives are not just mundane affairs, lived in day-to-day wasted drudgery. Instead, we must see that there is an acute need for holy times, sacred seasons, consecrated places, and sanctified experiences. So let's create holy things in our lives, and let's regain a sense of holiness in our hearts.

A good place to begin this purposeful pursuit could be the Lord's Day. Sabbath-keeping is all about a holy day. What a marvelous idea.* And so, what if...? What if we once again made the Lord's Day a holy day. We treated if differently. We made it special. What if we made it a day for worship? For rest? For fellowship? For refreshment? For renewal? For honoring God? What if for just one day out of seven we removed from our lives things like work? Business? Busyness? Shopping? Frantic rushing around? Stressful hurry? What if...? What if we took the Fourth Commandment seriously again?

Please understand what I am saying. I am not suggesting a legalistic commandeering of Sundays for religious purposes. To observe the Sabbath should not be a requirement, a bondage. Not now. Not this side of the Cross. But what about making it your personal, freely chosen purpose to do something different with your week, your time, your activity? Could this make a difference in your life? Would you get the rest you need? Would you have the time for family you never seem to find? Would it be meaningful to honor God with one day of your week? Would you live life differently if there were a holy time in your workaday schedule? Why not give it a try?

"I went to the place of public worship, lifting up my heart to God for assistance and grace, in my great work; and God was gracious to me, helping me to plead with him for holiness, and to use the strongest arguments with him, drawn from the incarnation and sufferings of Christ, for this very end, that men might be made holy." ~ David Brainerd, Diary, October 14, 1744.

*It is interesting to note that Brainerd himself used this tactic. In his diary entry for April 16, 1743, he records an encounter with some worldly-minded folk. He states, "discoursed about sanctifying the Sabbath" so as to "solemnize their minds."

Essay 8
Lords of Misrule

Lately I have seen a resurgence of a phenomenon that I first noticed about eight years ago, while I was living in Uniontown, PA. It is now occurring here in Crozet, the small community in central Virginia where I live, even as it did years ago in Pennsylvania. I remember what prompted my ire those many years ago. While driving through Uniontown first thing one morning, I came to a four-way intersection. As I approached this intersection with the intent of turning left, I encountered another motorist approaching from directly in front of me. We came to the intersection at almost precisely the same moment: I, with my left turn signal on; he, with no signal, indicating that he was coming straight through. Now, I am much older than I was when I first started driving. Indeed, I have spent a good portion of the past 3+ decades behind the wheel of an automobile. Yet, even so, I do not tend to suffer from either early dementia or vehicular amnesia. I still remember the basic rules of the road. For instance, in such a situation as I have described, the car that is going straight has the right of way. I, the lefty in this situation, must wait and yield the right of way. Simple stuff.

However, as I dutifully waited for this other car to proceed through the intersection, nothing happened. We both just sat there. After a moment of hesitation and wondering, I saw that the man across from me was beckoning for me to go ahead and turn. I wondered... why? There was no line of cars behind him. Indeed, we were the only cars at the intersection, or even in sight, for that matter. Waiting for him to go through the intersection was not a great hindrance to me. It meant waiting perhaps an additional two or three seconds. So why was he motioning me through?

Aahhh... I hear you sigh the answer... he was being nice. But was he? Perhaps. I could not read his mind or divine his motives. I only know that he irritated me. In fact, totally oblivious to what he was doing, he had stumbled upon one of my very worse pet peeves. He was giving up his vehicular right of way.

"So, what's the beef?" you say. Indeed, why do I feel so irritated by such a gracious gesture. Well, I plan on telling you.

What this man did had become a common practice there in Uniontown, even as it now is in Crozet. I don't know how it is in other parts of the country, but in our neck of the woods there is a virtual epidemic of people playing around with the traffic laws regarding right of way. It began a number of years ago, and has been increasing ever since. People come to intersections, hesitate, wait, and finally someone (it seems to usually be the person who actually has the right of way) motions for someone else to move.

This really bugs me. I know that this trend probably began as a matter of kindness on the part of some person or persons. But it has evolved into a troublesome problem. It has become so commonplace, that people seem to have forgotten what the rules of right of way were in the first place. If several cars approach an intersection at the same time there is a mild sense of tension that immediately arises. No one knows what to do. People wait. They look around. Some freeze in fear. Sometimes one person panics and bolts through the intersection. Chaos!

Now, we have all probably been kind to someone and let them go ahead of us in these kinds of situations. I have myself been at an intersection facing another car where I knew it was difficult to make a left hand turn. I have then waved that person ahead of me. You've done it too. Understandable. Kind. A Good Samaritan act. But when this is done unnecessarily, and repeatedly, it does indeed produce chaos. When drivers repeatedly begin to act outside the rules, making their own rules as they go, then everyone suffers. Instead of knowing what to anticipate as you draw near an intersection, you are confronted with uncertainty, apprehension, maybe even fear. (Think I exaggerate? I have looked at the faces of some fellow drivers and seen panic. They are terrified because they don't seem to know what to do, what is currently expected of them at an intersection.)

This phenomenon has become so widespread that it is becoming a real danger. I have seen several near accidents because two or three people were hesitating, then moving, then hesitating again, and then all moving again at an intersection. I have also seen situations where some people have come to expect that they will be allowed to go first. If you lawfully, reasonably, and rightfully proceed through an intersection in your turn, obeying the right-of-way laws, you may be placing your life in jeopardy. Someone else thinks they should go first, and they seize the right to proceed.

Yet, the traffic problems caused by this growing trend are not what bugs me the most. It is not what makes this one of my latest pet peeves. Rather, it is the underlying rationale that I think is operating here. Traffic flows in an orderly fashion when all drivers obey the laws of the road and each person operates within the parameters of mutually understood rules. But when people began to function according to individual rules and personal expectations, instead of group norms, there is disorder, even danger. It is the same way with society as a whole. When citizens of a nation perform the tasks of life within the confines of established laws, understood mores, and common rules, society functions in a safe and orderly manner. But when each individual begins to make up his or her own rules, and operate accordingly, then you never know what to expect. And this is the situation that is happening in our country today.

I have a feeling that not observing right-of-way traffic laws is only symptomatic of a much larger social ill. In our amoral, "each to his own" culture, societal norms and social rules are considered antiquated or passé. And worse, ordinary laws and long-established morals are viewed as unnecessary. They are certainly not to be considered binding (at least not on "me personally"). They are at best silly, and at worst constricting and enslaving. So say the postmodern prophets of chaotic freedom. Each man chooses for himself how to drive, where to park his car, when and how to turn... as well as, what is sexually moral, what constitutes legal marriage, and if it is okay to take another life (pre-born or post-born). In such a world, a la Sartre, it is equally moral and acceptable to give another man the right-of-way at an intersection or to pull out a gun and kill him for taking the right-of-way for himself. Conventions about kindness, or killing, don't matter anymore. I can kiss you or shoot you, the choice is wholly mine... and society's rules and laws are irrelevant.

I am afraid that we have become a nation of overgrown kids playing dress up. We don the external garb of sovereigns, and think we individually have the right to live as we please, make our own laws, and expect everyone else to dance to our moral tunes. We crown ourselves with self-delegated authority and assert our autonomy regarding God, the church, ethical behavior, social expectations… and reason. Masquerading as the 21st century lords of misrule, we forget that "…there is a way which seems right to a man, but in the end it leads to death" (Proverbs 14:12). In our puerile posing, we forget that we are attempting to usurp the place of the One who is sovereign, and who does rightfully give us laws and moral commands to follow. We have blinded ourselves to the fact that self-enthroned moral dictators will one day have to answer to the Judge of all the earth, and respond to His just and righteous demands. And our end will then be *sic simper tyrannis.*

Essay 9
"That's Not Nice." Good!

With the advent of an amoral, ethically apathetic, and increasingly characterless society—which we are now experiencing—we have correspondingly seen an epidemic spread through our land. There is a moral disease that is robbing us of convictions, values, and truthfulness. It is draining off our integrity, killing our sense of righteousness, and undermining the proclamation of truth. It is a sickness that rots the very fiber of our being as a nation, as a people. It is nothing less than a plague of NICENESS.

Niceness? Being nice? That's a moral illness? Yes, indeed. Lest you think I am exaggerating, allow me to cite a few examples that illustrate the gravity of the situation.

TRUTH MATTERS

Several years ago a couple came into my office at church. Their purpose was to ask me to marry them. However, I had some grave concerns about their relationship. First of all, I had found out that the woman was not legally divorced from her first husband. Second, she had lied to me about a number of issues. Third, I suspected that they were involved sexually. As they both claimed to be Christians (whatever they understood by the term), I felt that I must investigate these matters. So I questioned them.

When it came to the matter of their intimacy level, I asked them pointblank: "Are you having sex?" Their answer was an unashamed, blushless, direct "Yes." I then said, "Do you not know this is wrong? That it is a sin?" Their answer? Fasten your seatbelts for this one… They knew they were doing wrong. But it was really okay, because every morning they asked God to forgive them. I pressed them, trying to get them to see how wrong their attitudes were, as well as their actions. The woman became enraged that I was so mean as to not accept their lifestyle and their excuses. She stood, told me (and the man), "This conversation is over!" and stormed out of my office.

Later, word got back to me that she felt that "the pastor is not very nice." Hmmmmm.

Second example. Some time back I heard on the radio about a little girl in Huntington, WV who was mauled to death by a pit bull. Sad story. But perhaps just as sad is the fact that it could have been prevented. This dog had a history of attacking people. It had already seriously bitten at least four other people in the immediate neighborhood. However, none of these incidents had been reported. When one neighbor was asked why the authorities had not been informed about these attacks, he said, "Well, we are all such good neighbors, pretty close and all. We just didn't want to cause trouble for anyone." In other words, they were trying to be nice. Oh, how "nice" it was for that poor little girl!

Essay 9: *"That's Not Nice." Good!*

Another one...

At times we have all been shocked and horrified by what has happened in places devastated by floods, hurricanes or tornadoes. It makes me think of the aftermath of Hurricane Katrina. Our hearts were broken for the people in Louisiana, Mississippi and Alabama. Yet, as bad as the loss of life, the suffering, and the trauma were to all those poor people in New Orleans and elsewhere, they also had to also endure the shameful abuse of looters, thieves and low-down criminals. I can remember watching one news story about this terrible situation. A cable news camera crew videotaped three men looting a store. The men weren't embarrassed, ashamed or even afraid. They calmly went through a broken store window, came out loaded down with merchandise, and sauntered down the street as though it were just an ordinary day in the neighborhood. The reporter's take on the situation? He repeatedly talked about his surprise at how these "gentlemen" were behaving. That was his word: "gentlemen." My blood pressure shot up immediately. "Gentlemen!!!" Dear Father in heaven, help us! Now thieves, burglars, crooks, and low-life hoodlums are to be referred to as "gentlemen." Isn't this the epitome of the disease of niceness? Let's not offend anyone... even criminals.

Oh, by the way, my heart truly goes out to those who suffer in such situations. It is tragic when people have to do without food, water, shelter or medicine. I often pray that relief will come quickly to them. I give to help out, when I can. But let me say this about such situations. You will have a hard time convincing me that people who are stealing flat screen TV's and home entertainment centers are doing it out of desperation. I don't think that crooks who break into people's homes and take their personal belongings are simply frustrated because of the tragedy of their situation. (I know, this is not a nice thing to say.)

One final example...

I hate the way that the any public figure or politician who stands up for moral integrity and who has personal convictions is characterized as "petty," "partisan," or "uncompromising." Yes, for some this is indeed the case. And yes, there are too many politicians on both sides of the political divide who are purely partisan and act like spoiled children when they don't get their way. But there are others who are men and women of principle. And when they speak up about their values and beliefs they are castigated. Their offense? They don't play nice.

Do you see the ravages that this social epidemic is causing in our nation? It is no longer viewed as acceptable to be a person of moral conviction and principled character. To speak out in defense of truth and righteousness is not being "nice." Horrors. To say that some things are just plain wrong, wicked, or evil is looked upon as being the worst sin possible... the sin of not "playing nice."

Niceness is a funny thing. It claims to be loving... yet excuses sin, overlooks immorality, and winks at unrighteousness. Is this really loving? Is this showing concern for others?

Out of curiosity I looked it up. Do you know that the word "nice" is not used in the KJV, the New KJV, the NIV, or the NRSV. It is used once in the NASB in Jeremiah 12:6. Why the scarcity of "niceness" in the Bible?

Does the Bible enjoin us to be kind, compassionate, gentle, caring? Yes, most truly it does. But nowhere, NOWHERE, does it tell us to be nice. Indeed, many of the great servants of the Lord would be judged as not being very nice by today's standards. Think about these men:

- John the Baptist: "Brood of vipers. Who warned you to flee the wrath to come?" (Matt. 3:7). Oh no, John, don't say such things... that's not nice!

- Paul: "Son of the devil, you enemy of all righteousness, will you not cease perverting the straight ways of the Lord?" (Acts 13:10). Oh no, Paul, don't say such things... that's not nice!

- Jesus: "Woe to you, scribes and Pharisees, hypocrites! For you are like whitewashed tombs... Serpents, brood of vipers! How can you escape the condemnation of hell?" (Matt. 23:27, 33). Oh no, Jesus, don't say such things... that's not nice!

Now understand what I mean by this writing. I do not mean that we can excuse rudeness or being ill mannered. I do not mean that we can justify not being kind, patient, longsuffering, gentle, compassionate or tenderhearted. These things are required and obligatory upon Christian people. What I do mean is that we cannot use an attempt at being "nice" as an excuse for not standing by our convictions, speaking the righteous truth when it is needed, standing up for a moral position, or justifying wickedness and overlooking evil. To justify evil and to exonerate wickedness is just as bad as the evil and wickedness itself. See Malachi 2:17 and Isaiah 5:20.

Essay 10
Mother Earth Is Only a Child

I am foolish. I admit it. I have no qualms about saying it, confessing it. You see, I am foolish enough to believe that there are moral absolutes. I am foolish enough to believe that there is a God that rules in heaven and on earth. I am foolish enough to believe that the marriage covenant is sacred and should be inviolate. And, yes, I am foolish enough to believe that the Bible is trustworthy and accurate… even when it comes to such matters as the age of the earth itself.

"The age of the earth? You've got to be kidding!" Yes, I can hear your exclamation of surprise. I hear your tone of incredulity. "How can anyone be so naïve as to believe that the Bible is to be taken literally true and valid as regards the age of the earth? Hasn't modern science and reason demonstrated beyond a doubt that the earth is billions of years old?"

And my answer? Well, no, I really don't think that either science or reason has adequately demonstrated that the earth is billions of years old. But, I will not attempt in this essay to refute all the supposedly scientific evidence in favor of an old earth. Instead, I want to present a brief argument in favor of a young earth. This argument will attack the matter on three fronts: theological, philosophical and scientific. First, the theological...

THE BIBLE TELLS ME SO

Let's understand our terms first of all. By "young" I mean an age for the earth of somewhere around 6,000 to 10,000 years. This is quite a bit different from the popular view that the earth is anywhere from 4 to 5 billion years old. Quite a bit of difference indeed. Yet, it is this picture of a young earth which is presented to us in the Bible.

I must confess that if there were no other evidence for a young earth than the Biblical account, then that would be enough warrant for me to accept this view. I have the utmost confidence in the Biblical record. It has been substantiated repeatedly by archaeologists. It has been validated over and over again by historians. But even beyond this, even more basic than this, I have personally seen and experienced the supernatural power, the divine energy that is contained in this Book of books.

But how does the Bible fix the age of the earth at 6-10 thousand years? I hear you ask the question. It does so most notably through the genealogical tables found in Genesis, in 1 Chronicles, and in Luke. These tables record the lineage of the Patriarchs, the family of Abraham, and the family tree of Christ. In Genesis the genealogies actually give the ages of the people listed, ages which can be used

Essay 10: *Mother Earth Is Only a Child*

to calculate dates. Using these tables we can easily count backwards and determine that the creation is recorded as occurring about 4000 B.C. Now, some critics note that there may be gaps in these ancient records. And this may, admittedly, be true. However, even if there were large gaps, this would only add years, perhaps centuries to the dating. Furthermore, even if there were large enough gaps to add millennia, we are still talking about an earth that is no more than, say, 10,000 years old.

So, first of all, I believe the Biblical record... no, more than that, I am committed to and convinced of the truth of the Biblical record. And because I believe the Bible, I believe in a young earth.

There is a flip side to my theological argument. Most people probably think that the idea that the earth is very old is a newer, more modern concept. Their reasoning probably goes something like this: In ancient times, men believed that God (or the gods) created the earth in the very recent past. Now, through the advance of scientific thinking, we have come to realize that the earth is very, very old. Thus this is now the accepted, modern, scientific view.

I hate to burst your bubble, but the belief that the earth is very old is not a new idea at all. Indeed, many pagan and occult belief systems posit vast ages for the existence of nature. For example, in Hinduism, it is believed that the universe proceeds through huge periods of times, ages that last for many hundreds of thousands and even millions of years. We are presently in the dark age of Kali-Yuga, which has already lasted for 5000 years. Kali-Yuga has another 427,000 years to go. And this is only one age among many. Further, there are huge cycles of time called Brahma years, each of which lasts for millions and millions of years. Then, the cycle of time ends, and the entire scheme begins all over again. So you are talking about an earth that is billions and billions of years old.

The ancient Greeks also believed that time was essentially cyclical, that everything repeated itself over and over and over through tremendously long rounds of time. They thought that everything that now exists has existed before in the dim recesses of past ages, and will exist again in the recurring cycles of nature. For example, the Epicureans believed in an atomic view of reality. The basic building blocks of all reality, which they called "atoms" (not the same atoms as we believe in) form and reform themselves in many patterns. The possible combinations are vast in number, but still finite. As the atoms form, break apart, and reform, all possible existences come to be. We are now living in one possible combination of atoms. Some time in the future, this particular combination will dissolve and another formation will occur. Because there are a limited, though tremendously large, number of possible combinations of atoms, they will all occur over and over and over again. Everything exists in a continuous cycle of formation and reformation with no end to the recombinations.

And so it goes... the Theosophists believe in great ages that preceded the present time. Believers in Atlantis and Mu usually posit huge periods of time that preceded the current cycle of events. Buddhism asserts that we go through an almost endless series of rebirths stretched out over countless ages. Jainism says that there is no beginning or ending to existence, that all reality goes through countless cycles of birth, death, and rebirth over and over through millions of years.

Get the idea? The concept of a young earth, and existence itself being of recent origin, is not found in most religions or non-Christian belief systems. Actually, the very concept of linear time, in which time moves from a created beginning to a (purposeful) conclusion is of Biblical origin. It is in the Judeo-Christian heritage that we see this particular concept of time arise. Most pagan cultures accepted the concept of never ending cycles of existence that stretch out over millions of years.

MY MIND TELLS ME SO

My second reason for believing in a young earth is basically philosophical in nature. I was pondering this whole young earth issue recently, and a thought came to me. (A frightening occurrence, indeed!) I remember a philosophic concept from ancient Greece. Aristotle—you know the guy, pupil of Plato and tutor of Alexander—well, he developed an idea that he called *entelecheia*, or entelechy, as we render it in English. The concept of entelechy involves the end product, the goal of something. Fundamentally, the idea is this. What something will become is contained in that thing from the beginning. The end goal of an acorn is an oak tree. So all that an acorn needs to become an oak tree is contained in the acorn, and the very make-up of the acorn is determined beforehand by the oak tree. You might say, the end determines the means. You also might say that the goal necessitates the process. What something has been, or is now, is wholly dependent on what it will become.

Now, this might seem a little strange to you, but actually the idea can dovetail with a Biblical worldview very nicely. If we accept the notion (as I do) of a Sovereign Omnipotence who runs the universe according to a divine plan and purpose, then we must accept that all that exists is working toward a goal. And we can further accept that the process, the "getting there" if you will, is determined by that end result. What exists, and what happens, is occurring because God is working all things out according to His plan and to achieve His purpose. (Consider the following verses: Ephesians 1:11, Romans 8:28, Eph. 2:4-7, Isaiah 41:4, Isa. 48:3, Prov. 16:4)

Now, allow me to apply the concept of entelechy to our argument. To do this, I ask you to consider these questions: What is the end product of creation? What is the goal of reality? Where do we see everything headed... and by that "everything" we include the cosmos, history, nature, and mankind? The answer is pretty evident from Scripture. The goal of the universe is redeemed humanity living in a love relationship with the Triune God and existing to serve His glory. Basically it boils down to this: God and the church, Christ and His Bride. Now applying the principle of entelechy, we would have to conclude that all that exists, all history, all of the myriad and various workings of nature, all reality, all these together have this one purpose: Christ's plan for His redeemed Bride. The goal (the Bride) determines the means (nature, history, the cosmos).

Now, let us take our argument a step further. If you consider the original creation of mankind, the divine mandate in the Garden, and then the Fall, and the plan of redemption... well, you can see how God has worked through all this to bring about His ultimate purpose. But, and this is the key point here, how would millions and billions of years of non-human existence serve this goal? If the entelechic process results in a redeemed Bride for the Savior, what purpose does eons of time without any humans serve? And what purpose is there in the process of evolution itself? All these prior ages, and all inorganic and organic processes that existed billions of years before mankind have no purpose in redemption! Therefore, they are meaningless. Would the Sovereign Lord of the universe waste His time like this? I think not. He even tells us that the earth was created for men (Isaiah 45:18-19)—not amoeba, trilobites, dinosaurs, mastodons, or lemurs. Indeed, the very idea of entelechy, and God's purpose being behind the created order, is explicit in Scripture (e.g., see Isaiah 46:8-10). Thus, the idea that God has a purpose and plan for all history—whose end goal is redeemed humanity loving and serving the Creator—

necessitates a cosmic history that does not exclude mankind from the bulk of that history itself.

SCIENCE TELLS ME SO

My third reason for believing in a young age of the earth is found in the halls of scientific endeavor. Most people believe that science "proves" that the earth is about 4.5 billion years old. They assume that it is a verifiable fact that things have been around for a long, long, long time. But is this so?

First of all, you need to understand that contemporary secular science posits the NEED for an old earth because evolution could not occur unless this is so. But this is more a philosophical stance, rather than a scientific one. Secondly, it is usually asserted that there are demonstrable scientific evidences for a universe that is eons old, e.g., radioactive dating methods. However, these dating methods are not without their own problems. They assume a lot, such as the amount of radioactive material present originally, the rate of decay being constant, etc. Also, they have been proven to be unreliable at times, and sometimes completely false. But, I won't belabor this side of the issue. What I would like to do is to briefly consider just a few of the scientific reasons for believing in a young earth. These are sort of cosmic "clocks," if you will.

Erosion: We can measure the rate at which erosion is wearing down the earth's surface, especially mountains. Erosion actually occurs rather rapidly. This rate of erosion is much higher than the rate of any forces which tend to build up mountains. If the earth were billions of years old the mountains should not exist—for they should have all been worn down ages ago.

Magnetic Field: The earth's magnetic field is decaying at a measurable rate. If the earth were billions of years old, by now we would have no magnetic field. Also, working backward in time, and using the known rate of decay, if the earth were even millions of years old, the magnetic field in the far past would have been so great that nothing could have evolved and lived. The current rate of decay indicates that a reasonable age for the earth must be measured in the 1000's of years, not billions.

Human Population: At the current rate of population growth, we could have arrived at our present population in about 4000 years. This fits in well with the Flood account of Genesis. However, if the human population were many 10's of thousands, or even millions or years old, then there wouldn't be room to contain the many billions of people who would be living now.

Receding Moon: The moon is gradually moving away from the earth, at the rate of around 2 inches per year. At the current rate, 2 billion years ago the moon and the earth would have been touching. (Remember, the earth is supposed to be 4.5 billion years old.) Further, if the earth were 4-5 billion years old, then the moon should be so far away by now that you could not even see it. Bye-bye, man on the moon!

Oil Pressure: Ever seen one of those old movies where someone out West strikes oil and a gusher erupts. The gusher occurs because the oil is under great pressure. However, it has been demonstrated this is pressure is gradually dissipating, sort of like a slow leak in your car tire. If the earth were more than about 7000 years old then there would no pressure to force the oil to erupt as it does. It wouldn't be a gusher, it would just be an oozer.

Comet disintegration: Evolutionists believe that comets were formed along with the solar system, about 4 to 5 billion years ago. However, every time a comet passes near the sun, some of it is swept away by solar forces. At the present rate, comets cannot be more than

100 million years old. This is a far cry from 6,000 years... but it is even a farther cry from 4.5 billion!

Helium: All radioactive decay processes result in helium being released into the atmosphere. But consider this: There is no known way for helium to escape the earth's atmosphere. However, there is only enough helium to account for about 10,000 years of radioactive decay, and that is assuming that all helium has resulted from such sources. Conclusion: the earth cannot be billions of years old.

And the evidences go on and on...

Indeed, I have only listed a few of the many evidences for a young earth. Want more? Check out Answers in Genesis at answersingenesis.org or Creation Ministries at creation.com.

And so, dear reader, you see that I am a fool, and I take a fool's position on the age of the earth. But with the Bible, philosophy, and science on my side, I don't think my position is such a bad place to be. What do you think?

Essay 11
Here Is Your God!

In Exodus 32, we see a very sad story. In the many sad stories of the idolatrous and wayward history of the people of Israel, this is surely one of the most tragic. Here we see Israel just six weeks after the awesome display of God's power in delivering them from Egypt. With that dramatic memory still burning within them, they begin to question Moses and God. In Exodus 32:1, they express wonder that Moses, who is on Mt. Sinai receiving the tables of the Law, has been gone so long. They also have seen God just recently manifest His glory and presence in the fire, smoke, thunder and quaking of the mountain. Yet, despite all this, they are questioning not just Moses, but God Himself. And so they demand of Aaron, "Make us a god who will go before us!"

So what did poor, foolish Aaron do? He bowed to the will of crowd. He made them an idol, a golden calf. And when they saw it, they declared, "This is your god, O Israel, who brought you up from the land of Egypt." Wait a minute… THIS is your god? Yes. They said that this golden calf, this idol made by men's hands, is nothing less than Jehovah God Himself. They declared that this image was the Lord God, their Deliverer and Savior.

The word used for "god" here is Elohim. This is a common word for the Lord in the Old Testament. It is in the plural, and in the correct context may be rendered as "gods." You will notice that many translations render it as "gods" in this passage. However, it is evident from this context that the Israelites were not making "gods," rather they were making a "god," just one idol. And they said that this was "the god" who had brought them out of Egypt (32:4, 8). Further, when Aaron saw the response of the people, he proclaimed a feast, a worship celebration for Jehovah/Yahweh (32:5). The evidence is clear—they called this idol by the name of the Lord God, Yahweh Elohim. But just because you call an idol "Elohim" or "God" does not make it really God.

How utterly sad! And yet, are we any different today? How many times do we hear the strident voices of the ecclesiastical world proclaiming to us, "This is your god!"—when it is not God at all. There are so many, far too many, instances of a false god, an idol, being promoted as the God of Christianity. And in reality it is only an image, somebody's imagined perception of the deity. And just because you call your false deity "God" or "the Lord" does not make it really God.

Consider some examples of what I am saying:

- "God is love and He never judges or punishes sin."
  … THIS is your god!

- "God loves all people, therefore he accepts and approves all lifestyles."
  … THIS is your god!

Essay 11: *Here Is Your God!*

- "God would never send anybody to hell. Therefore, hell can't be real."
  ...THIS is your god!

- "God is cruel and harsh. He delights in punishing sinners."
  ...THIS is your god!

- "If you suffer, it is because you have sinned. God is punishing you."
  ... THIS is your god!

- "God wants His children to be wealthy and healthy. So if you are in need, it is your own fault. You have a lack of faith."
  ... THIS is your god!

- "I don't believe God is all that concerned about doctrine. God does not require absolutes."
  ... THIS is your god!

- "It doesn't matter what you call Him—God, Allah, Krishna, whatever—they are all different names for the same God."
  ... THIS is your god!

- "I don't need God. I am okay on my own. I can take care of myself."
  ...THIS is your god!

- "A little sin is okay. God is not really that strict about morality."
  ... THIS is your god!

- "You've sinned. So just give up. God sees you as a total failure."
  ... THIS is your god!

- "You can get to heaven without being a Christian. Jesus is just one of many ways."
  … THIS is your god!

- "Just so you try hard, that's all it takes to get to heaven. God doesn't expect perfection."
  …THIS is your god!

- "You can't call Mormons or Jehovah's Witnesses or other such groups 'cults.' That is not being kind. We are all Christians."
  … THIS is your god!

- "Just so you love Jesus, it doesn't matter what you believe about Him."
  …THIS is your god!

- "Nobody understands the Trinity anyway. Why would we have to believe in something we can't understand."
  … THIS is your god!

- "There are many paths to God. There are many roads to heaven."
  … THIS is your god!

And the list could go on and on. In the spiritual climate we live in today, we could spend quite a long time cataloging all the false gods that people worship. And sad to say, so utterly sad, is that far too many people are sitting in church pews on Sunday mornings thinking they are good Christians, but in their hearts they are worshipping a golden calf. They are bowing to an idol which they think of as the true God of the Christian faith.

In our clamoring to be like the world (see Ezekiel 20:32), to be accepted by the world, we have rejected the true God for a host of golden calves. We have set up a false god and thought to ourselves that we are okay—because we have said, "This is my God. This is Elohim, the true God." But it is not. It is an idol. It is a false image. It is a replacement for God. Remember, just because you call your false deity "God" or "the Lord" does not make it really God. (See Jeremiah 2:11-13.)

Is there hope for us today? Is there hope for America? For the West? Yes. But it is found in one thing, and one thing only. If we return to the God of our Fathers, the true God of the Bible, then we may yet see God turn things around. If not… then I fear for our land.

Essay 12
Is the Belief in the Trinity Necessary?

I have sometimes heard statements made by Christians that go something like this: "The Bible doesn't explicitly teach the Trinity. And there is so much controversy about this. Do you have to believe in the Trinity to be saved? Or isn't belief in Jesus enough to be a Christian? Do we really have to make a big deal over the Trinity?"

Well, what do you think? I have no qualms about telling you my answer. Simply put, YES, belief in the Trinity is an essential doctrine of the faith. You cannot be a genuine believer in Jesus and deny the Holy Trinity. But let's elaborate a little—and see if this is biblically true.

We live in a day when essential Christian doctrines are being questioned more and more frequently. And the biblical doctrine of the Triune God is no different. This is a question of crucial importance. First of all, let's address the statement that "the Bible doesn't explicitly teach the Trinity." It is true that the technical language about the Trinitarian nature of God as found in the creeds of the church, such as the Nicene and Athanasian Creeds, are not found explicitly in the Bible. However, this does not mean that there are no clear-cut Scriptural passages that present a definite teaching about God as a Triune Being. The more you study both the Old and New Testaments, the more clearly you will see a distinctly straightforward understanding of God as being both One and Three. Indeed, it was because this truth was so evident to the early church that they spent centuries studying, debating, discussing, and coming to grips with how to clearly define and understand what the Scriptures plainly presented. Thus, over time we came to have the carefully chosen words of creeds, as well as clear expositions of the doctrine by many of the Church Fathers. The truth came first—the technical and defining language came afterwards.

Okay, so let's say we accept that the Bible does teach the Trinity. But this is an admittedly challenging doctrine to grasp and explain. So is it worth it? Is it even necessary? If a person understands the basics of who Jesus is, what He did in His atoning work, and that His redemptive plan has provided salvation for us—is this not enough? Can't someone be saved and not accept the doctrine of the Trinity?

First of all, please understand that I fully accept that salvation is by grace. And I do not limit His grace. Salvation is not based on intellectual knowledge and understanding. Yet, knowing the truth is an essential feature of the faith. There are some ideas, concepts, and teachings that you simply have to believe if you are to be a Christian. And knowing the true God is one of them.

Essay 12: *Is the Belief in the Trinity Necessary?*

Jesus said that eternal life consists in knowing the true God and the true Christ (John 17:3). If you give this just a moment's thought you will see that it makes sense. In Evangelical circles we often say that Christianity is more about a relationship than it is about religion. Coming into a personal relationship with Christ is a large part of what it means to become a Christian. Understanding this truth then begs the question: Is it not necessary to have a relationship with the right God, and the right Christ? If you enter into a relationship with a false god or a false messiah, how can you say that you have a true salvation experience? A true saving relationship?

And who is the true God? Who is the true Christ? The answer is certain. The God of the Bible is a Triune Being.[1] The Christ of the Scriptures is God the Son, Second Person of the Trinity.[2] There is no other God and there is no other Christ—and it is only in knowing Him/Them that you have eternal life.

It is also noteworthy to consider what the Apostle John said in 2 John 1:9. He declares that "anyone who does not abide in the doctrine of Christ does not have God." It is unclear in the original whether the phrase "the doctrine of Christ" means the doctrine that Christ taught or the doctrine about Christ. But for the purpose of our discussion, either understanding is appropriate. Among the many things Christ taught is a clear assertion of Trinitarian truth. And when we consider the writings about Christ, as found in the rest of the New Testament, again the Trinity shines forth brightly. In other words, one of the plain teachings both by Christ and about Christ is that of the Trinity. Thus, to reject this specific teaching is to reject essential, necessary doctrine. And John declares that to reject such teaching is to reject God Himself. You cannot have God, truly know Him, and believe false things about Him.

We should also consider the active roles of each member of the Godhead in all divine endeavors. A careful study of the Bible demonstrates that all three Persons were operational in creation.[3] The Bible says that all three Persons were involved in Christ's Resurrection—Father,[4] Son[5] and Spirit.[6] All three Persons worked (and presently work) in the plan of bringing salvation to mankind.[7] All three Persons are active in the life of the believer—sanctifying,[8] establishing,[9] empowering,[10] nurturing, helping, guiding, and aiding in his maturing process. All three Persons are involved in a believer's prayer life.[11] All three Persons are deserving of worship, and participate in the believer's worship experience.[12] God as One and God as Three is/are present, effective, and engaged in all that happens in both the spiritual and natural worlds. He is at work. They are at work. So how can you deny the reality of this Triune Being and yet believe in the true Christian faith?

Paul said that "in Him we live and move and have our being" (Acts 17:28). All of existence is wrapped up in His being. There is nothing that exists apart from Him. There is nothing that can be real without having its very being derived from His reality. He is truly the underlying substance of the universe. And He is God who is One, and God who is Three. Can we deny Him in regard to His own self-revealed identity and yet still claim to know Him, to have a saving relationship with Him? This is not only unbiblical, it is illogical. Indeed, it is more than illogical, it is ludicrous. He has revealed Himself as the Three-in-One Deity. To deny His self-revelation as the Trinity is to reject God Himself, as He truly exists.

But what about someone, say a new Christian, who is ignorant of this doctrine. What about that person? Let's address this issue. If someone has enough understanding to grasp salvation by grace and the work of Christ, then he can be saved. And if initially he is ignorant of the true biblical teaching about God, then we cannot limit God's grace in this situation. However, ignorance is not a state a Christian should abide in. And as a believer grows in his relationship with Christ, he should and will grow in his understanding of who His Lord is—including His Trinitarian nature.

The fact of the matter is this. The doctrine of the Trinity is fundamental to the Christian faith. Yes, belief in the Trinity is necessary in order to be a true believer in Jesus. Furthermore, if anyone has a true knowledge of the nature of God, understands the doctrine of the Triune Deity, and rejects this biblical truth, then he is a genuine heretic. Such a person has placed himself outside the doctrinal boundaries that define what it means to "know the true God and Jesus Christ" whom the Father has sent (cf. John 17:3 again).

REFERENCES

1. Matthew 28:19, 2 Corinthians 13:14, Deuteronomy 6:4, Genesis 1:26, Isaiah 48:16.

2. John 8:58, John 1:1-3, John 10:30, 1 John 5:20, Hebrews 1:8, Titus 2:13.

3. Genesis 1:1, Isaiah 64:8, Malachi 2:10, Genesis 1:2, Psalm 104:30, Job 33:4, Psalm 33:6, Colossians 1:16-17, John 1:3, Hebrews 1:2.

4. Acts 2:24, Acts 13:30

5. John 2:19, John 10:18

6. Romans 1:4, Romans 8:11, I Peter 3:18

7. All three are seen as working in salvation in Ephesians 1:3-14, Galatians 4:4-6, 1 Peter 1:2, and scattered throughout Romans 8. In addition, there are numerous verses throughout the New Testament mentioning the work of each Person of the Godhead in His individual role in salvation.

8. Romans 15:16, 1 Peter 1:2, John 17:17, 1 Thess. 5:23-24, 1 Corinthians 1:2, 1 Corinthians 1:30, Hebrews 10:10 & 14.

9. 2 Corinthians 1:21-22.

10. Acts 1:8, Luke 24:49, Matthew 28:18-20, Luke 10:19.

[11] We pray to the Father, in the name of the Son, through the agency of the Holy Spirit. Cf. Ephesian 2:18, Jude 1:20-21.

[12] Note Ephesians 5:18-20. Worship of the Father is obvious. The Son was often worshiped even while here on earth: Matthew 14:33, 28:9, 17; John 9:38. As God, the Spirit is certainly deserving of worship. The explicit worship of the Holy Spirit would emerge later in church history.

Essay 13
If by Chance…

In discussing the theory of evolution, I have often mentioned the fact that the processes of organic evolution are all random events. Contrary to the idea of a Creator who designed the cosmos, evolution is squarely based on chance. However, I have been taken to task for this assertion. The objection I have heard is this: Natural Selection is not a random process. This is the position of noted scientist (and atheist) Richard Dawkins. Dawkins asserts that natural selection is a "non-random force." He says there is an inherent determinism in natural selection. Multitudes of generations of genetic selection have caused the inevitable survivability of a species. There is a natural design and order in this process. My question is this: Is natural selection, and thus Darwinian evolution itself, something that is deterministic and non-random or is it truly random?

Let's for a moment assume that Dawkins is right (an assumption that makes me shudder and causes bile to rise in my mouth). Let's assume there is an orderly, genetically pre-determined process to natural selection. Assuming that evolution is true, let's imagine that we are presented with two feline creatures on the way to becoming true tigers. Let's call these proto-tigrine creatures T-1 and T-2. Now T-1 has been born with slightly different musculature than T-2. T-1 is faster and more agile than the other. It is more naturally fitted to survive and thrive.

Like modern tigers, these tigrine creatures are solitary hunters. So T-1 is more proficient in the hunt, better at bringing down his prey. T-1 has a better chance of survival than T-2. Now imagine that food is scarce. Normally these tigerish animals stay within their own territories, but hunger drives them to find food wherever possible. Eventually they both smell the scent of a proto-deer (who happens to be named Bambi). They both stalk their prey. T-1, being better fitted for the hunt, brings down this cervine beast first. Not willing to share (tigers are notoriously selfish creatures—just ask Shere Khan) T-1 will not allow T-2 any of the kill. T-1 gorges himself and lives to hunt another day. T-2 goes away hungry. Weary from malnutrition, he collapses in the shade of a rock, and is eaten alive by Kaaaa (distance ancestor of Kaa). According to Dawkins, this is not a random occurrence. This moment in the natural selection process has been fixed in place by generations of genetic modifications over the millennia of evolution that has engendered these two specific proto-tigrines. And the end result of all that evolutionary effort is the inevitable survival of T-1 and the death of T-2. Non-random. Determined. Neat, tidy and logical.

Right. Right?

Let's reconsider this. Even if we assume that natural selection is a non-random, determined process (which I do not), we must also

Essay 13: *If by Chance...*

recognize that there are any number of other factors at work in this scenario. To illustrate, let's consider some alternative scenes.

Both T-1 and T-2 caught the scent of Bambi. But what if the wind had shifted just a bit and T-1 did not smell the beast? Result: T-1 goes hungry and dies. Cause of event: Chance.

What if T-1 were to step in a hole and break his leg? T-2 makes the kill. Result: T-1 goes hungry and dies. Cause of event: Chance.

What if a herd of elephants just happened to come by and slowed down T-1's approach of Bambi? Result: T-1 goes hungry and dies. Cause of event: Chance.

What if Bambi fell off a cliff on the way to the "rendezvous point." Neither predator gets to eat. Result: T-1 and T-2 both go hungry and die. Cause of event: Chance.

What if that herd of elephants got spooked and stampeded? The herd runs down poor Bambi. Neither predator gets to eat. Result: T-1 and T-2 both go hungry and die. Cause of event: Chance.

What if Bambi were not alone? What if there were several deer, and both predators get to eat?

Result: T-1 and T-2 both survive. Cause of event: Chance.

And consider this... what was it that brought T-1's parents together to mate and produce this genetically determined superior hunter in the first place? How many different random events occurred that caused this to happen—or how many events could have occurred that have prevented their union. Bottom line: Chance.

What if.... Well, you get the idea. We could go on and on spinning a myriad of possible tales. The point is that genetics is not the only factor involved in this scenario, in any such scenario. There are many varied factors. And each one is a contributing determiner of the final outcome. And each one is caused by pure chance, "non-random" genetics notwithstanding.

Even Dawkins admits this. In speaking of the branching that occurs in the development of the "evolutionary tree" he says this: "Each branching event is called a speciation: a breeding population splits into two, and they go their separately evolving ways. Among sexually reproducing species, speciation is said to have occurred when the two gene pools have separated so far that they can no longer interbreed. Speciation begins by accident."[1] Note the last sentence. What causes a branch to occur, speciation to happen? Accident.

If there is no Creator, no Designer, no Mind with an overarching purpose then there is no assurance of anything. All is random. All occurs by chance.

All? Yep. All.

Take it back further. As evolutionists would have it, mammals have become the dominant species on this planet because of the extinction of the dinosaurs. Why did this happen? No one knows for sure. Currently the most common theory is that a comet smashed into the earth about 65 million years ago, resulting in a planetary catastrophe which killed off the dinosaurs. Ever think about that event? What caused this particular comet to strike this particular planet in the first place? Was its trajectory nudged by passing near Jupiter, feeling the tug of that giant planet's gravity? Was its path affected by interactions with other comets, asteroids, or just a multitude of bits of space detritus? We can't reckon how many chance events resulted in this specific comet crashing into this specific planet.

Go back further still. If the evolutionist is right, then several billion years ago several molecules came together at just the right time, in just the right combination, in just the right environment to form some primeval proto-amino acids... which later would just happen to come together at just the right time, in just the right combination, in just the right environment to form some primeval amino acids... which later would just happen to come together at just the right time, in just the right combination, in just the right environment to form some primeval proteins... which later would just happen to come together at just the right time, in just the right combination, in just the right environment to form the necessary organic materials for life... which later.... Well, again, you get the picture.

Maybe (a BIG maybe) Dawkins might be right about natural selection. But natural selection is only one piece of a very large puzzle. Very large. Say, millions and billions of pieces. And it has all come together to the finished product we see today, activated and carried out by nothing more than random processes and chance occurrences.

What a different world this is from the Christian world. A different world entirely! In our world there is a Creator who sovereignly and omnisciently planned and ordered everything. Everything was purposefully designed as a piece of this huge puzzle, and fits just right because the divine Designer meant for it to fit. Nothing is random. Nothing was left to chance. There is meaning and purpose to each piece, and to the whole. And that means there is meaning and purpose for your existence!

REFERENCE

[1] Dawkins is quoted at http://www.noanswersingenesis.org.au/dawkins_evolution.htm.

Essay 14
Does Theology Matter?

Does theology matter? If you listen to some people, you would have to say, "No!"

For example, a few weeks ago I was talking with a friend who is taking some classes in theology. He told me how excited he was in his studies. He also told me that he shared his excitement with a friend. His friend commented positively, but then said, "But really, in the grand scheme of things, what does all that matter? In our everyday lives, what good is theology?"

My friend was telling me this to make the point that theology is okay for theologians, philosophers, and academicians. But for the common man, living in the real world, it has no value.

He went on to tell me that talking with this man reminded him of a time in this person's life when he was really struggling. He was going through a period of great hurt, much suffering. What kept him going? What encouraged him to not quit? It wasn't theology. It was the love, support and caring concern of Christian friends around him. Obviously, theology is a good thing—but what value does it have in the "real world" in everyday life? Implicit answer: None.

Whoa! Back up a minute. I couldn't disagree more. Theology and Christian doctrine are not esoteric studies for a few scholars in some academic lofty towers. They are the very stuff of "real life." Let me give you a prime example…

Let's look again at this man who went through such a challenging period in his life. What kept him going? Love. The love of the saints.

But wait a minute, where does love come from? There is a simple answer: "Love comes from God" (1 John 4:7 NIV) and "We love because He first loved us" (1 John 4:19 NIV). Love originates with God. It comes from God. It comes from Him because He IS love (1 John 4:16).

And that is the point. The Christian faith teaches us that God is love. This is a distinctive statement about our God. Islam doesn't teach this. Hinduism doesn't teach this. Buddhism doesn't teach this. Only Christianity teaches that God is love; that it is an essential feature of His very Being.

Why is this true? How can Christians say that God is love? Even religions that emphasis love and compassion (e.g., Buddhism) do not say that God is love. Why? Again, the answer is simple. Our God is triune in nature. In the oneness of His being He exists as a trinity of three divine Persons. And these three Persons have existed in a loving relationship for all eternity. No solitary being could be called "love." You cannot say Allah is love. He exists alone, solitary, by himself. Love requires an object. Only a multi-personal deity can love, and exist as love itself. Only of the Triune God can it be said that "God is love."

Essay 14: *Does Theology Matter?*

Look again at the last couple of paragraphs. What have we been discussing? Theology! (Oh, no! Not that!) See what I mean, theology is extremely practical. The very love that encouraged and helped that man in his suffering could only exist because of the triune God. No Trinity, no God who is love. No divine love, NO love at all. Love only exists at all because of the Triune Deity. And we can only understand, appreciate and fully practice this love if we know and understand Him. And that, my friend, is theology.

Essay 15
The Self-Contradiction of Evolution

This morning I have been reading the latest issue of *National Geographic* magazine (July 2015). In one of the small half-page features that NG has near the beginning of the magazine there is found the tale of the quagga mussel. Quagga mussels are a species native to the Ukraine. They have apparently been hitching rides as stowaways in the ballasts of ocean-going ships and have made their way to the U.S. Now this invasive species is over-running the Great Lakes. The quagga mussels are eating up native algae and changing the entire ecosystem of the Lakes. You know what I say? So what?

"Wait a minute," I hear you cry. "Don't you care that an entire ecosystem is in danger of being destroyed?"

Well, actually I do. I care about the environment. I care about the earth. I believe responsible Christian believers should care. God is the Creator of this planet, and He gave earth into the hands of man to steward and care for it. Yes, I do care. But I responded with a facetious "So what?" because of evolutionary theory. You see, evolution is all about survival. Period. That's it. Any organic life found in the Ukraine (or the Great Lakes) has developed so that it is capable of survival when other species have not—and that is simply the stuff evolution is made of. There is no moral issue here. There can be no moral issue in evolution. What survives is good, right and it is what is supposed to be dominant in any ecosystem. That's it. So, GO quagga! Yea!

You see, you can't have it both ways. You can't posit that the evolutionary process (chance organic modifications, random mutations, and evolutionary survivability) is what is supposed to happen and then complain when it does happen. So what if you like the former Great Lakes ecosystem? Too bad. Evolution means changes in organisms and, over the long haul, dramatic changes in organisms. And modified and different organisms will automatically result in changes in food chains, species extinction, and different ecosystems. It is the nature of evolution.

Isn't it funny that we want evolution to be this grand, wonderful, inexorable process that is responsible for all that lives on this planet—but we don't like it in certain specific instances. So... get over it. This is just the way it is. There is no moral mandate here. There is no design or purpose to nature. There is no overarching plan for the planet. What happens is just what happens. It is the way of nature. Get used to it—if you truly believe in evolution.

It is the same thing when it comes to GMO's, genetically modified organisms. Many people concerned with healthy eating now want us to shun these bugaboos. But wait a minute.... Isn't this

Essay 15: *The Self-Contradiction of Evolution*

what evolution is all about? Aren't genetically modified organisms the very part and parcel of evolutionary theory? Indeed, some biologists assert that the evolutionary process occurs through a series of fits and starts. It is called punctuated equilibrium. Basically this means that BIG random mutations occur every so often that bring radical changes in evolutionary development. It is in this way the fittest survive and organic progress is made. It is the very stuff of evolution. And each advance is simply a naturally occurring GMO. So what's the big deal if human beings are doing the same thing that nature has been doing for millions of years. Same thing, isn't it? Again, there is no moral issue here. What happens, just happens.

Indeed, couldn't you assert that if humans advance their own species through GMO's then this is a good thing? Haven't we evolved to be the species we are? So you could argue that our superior intelligence that enables us to understand genetic theory and to modify the genetic process is just part of our evolutionary "destiny." To do this is just the natural result of the evolutionary process for homo sapiens.

Unless.... Unless we are morally responsible. Unless we are truly stewards of this planet. Unless there is a God who created all things with a purpose. Unless evolution is a myth, creationism makes sense, and we do have a Maker that we will answer to. And we will answer to Him in regards to how we treated the planet He made, and that He placed us in charge of keeping for Him (see Genesis 1:26, 2:15 and Revelation 11:18). If this is true (as I firmly believe it is), then there is a reason for being concerned about quagga mussels, as well as any other environmental concerns. We care about these things because all life has been placed here by design, by a Creator. All life, and all ecosystems, and this planet itself are part of His plan. They have meaning and purpose, and they have value. There is no meaning, no value, in evolutionary theory. There is only survivability. If you want moral value and ethical environmental responsibility, then I would suggest that you examine your theory of origins. It makes all the difference.

Essay 16
Moldy Evolutionary Cake

Theistic evolution is a classic example of wanting to have your cake and eat it too. If you are not familiar with the theory, it is basically this: God is the Creator of all things, but evolution is the means He used to bring about all organic life on earth. So, according to this theory, the earth is billions of years old. Life began spontaneously in some primordial oceanic goo millions of years ago. The generally accepted secular geological time table is correct. And human beings are evolved primates, descended from some ape-like ancestor of a few million years ago.

Theistic evolutionists who are Christians (are there non-Christian examples?) generally accept the moral and theological truths of the Bible. They believe in God, the Trinity, the Deity of Christ, the bodily resurrection of the Lord, salvation through grace, and other essential doctrines of the Christian faith. They simply reject a straightforward interpretation of the early chapters of Genesis as literal and historic.

Now I think there are a number of problems with this view. Chief among them is this: To reject the Genesis accounts of the Creation, early human history, and the Flood is dangerous. When you reject any portion of Scripture at your own choosing, you call into question the entire rest of Scripture. Indeed, you cast doubt on the Bible as a whole. But this is not what I want to deal with today. I want to focus on one other problem in the theistic evolutionary view.

If theistic evolutionary theory is true, then life has been around for millions of years. Through the long ages of its history, this planet has seen myriads of creatures live and then die. There have been innumerable carnivores that have spent their lives pursuing, killing, and then eating innumerable herbivores. Disease, plague, accidents and injuries have been the norm for thousands of millennia. The world has suffered through countless hurricanes, typhoons, tornadoes, tsunamis, earthquakes, floods, and global climate changes. In other words, for eons there has been pain, suffering, destruction, and death on this planet.

Pretty obvious, right? But if you believe in God, and you believe in the Bible, and you also believe that God has used natural processes over millions of years to effect the evolution of all life—well, how are you to explain all this death and destruction? All these of these things (disease, accidents, tornadoes, etc.) are what are called "natural evils." They are evils. They are not good things. But there is no moral or spiritual content to them. They are just natural. They just happen. They are "natural evils."

The traditional biblical view offers a ready solution to the issue of natural evil. Adam was created as the apex of God's creative process. When Adam rebelled and fell away from God, then all of creation suffered as a consequence. From Romans 8:21-23 we understand that the creation itself has been brought into corruption and bondage. Here we see the image of creation groaning and crying out for redemption, which will only be realized in the resurrection and coming restoration of all things. It is the Fall of Adam that brought about natural evil.

It is also in the Fall that we understand the origin of death itself. Death came about as a result of sin (see Genesis 2:17, Romans 5:12). Before the Fall, there was no sin. And without sin, there was no death. The two are tied together.

Most theistic evolutionists (that I have ever read) do seem to believe in a Fall. They believe that things happened sort of like this. Evolution eventually produced a human being who was capable of entering into a spiritual relationship with God. This evolved being was "Adam." God put a human spirit in this evolved Adam-creature. Yet, this Adam-creature somehow fell into sin. End result: the Fall. And the Fall produced the spiritual and natural evils we now must endure. But one question lingers. If this is true, how do you explain the death of all living things before this Fall?

Indeed, how does theistic evolution explain these two realities at all: natural evil and death? I don't know. I can only think of two possibilities. One is that God is the origin of these things. As Creator, He made the world as it is. This means that He must have created it with natural evil inherent in it. Then this is the way God intended for things to be. Is God then the origin of disease, disaster, pain, suffering, and death? Is this the God of the Bible we worship and serve? Emphatically NO! Yes, God is seen in Scripture as using these things. But they are clearly not part of His original creation, and were not His initial intention for the world. In the book of Genesis, chapters 1 and 2, we see God create a beautiful world, a perfect environment, that is not only "good" but "very good." To posit that all natural evil was the intended creative work of God is an affront to God Himself.

The only other possibility I see is that we must trace everything back to Satan and his fall. At first glance, this seems plausible. Death, destruction, and evil certainly are the result of sin. And Satan's rebellion against God was certainly sinful. So could this be the answer?

Not really. First of all, there is absolutely no biblical support for this theory. Secondly, you would have to rethink all of the Scriptures that point to Adam as the source of sin and death in this world. Thus, you would need to rethink a whole lot of the Bible! The Scriptures never attribute the current world situation to the Devil. Instead, it is consistently laid at the feet of Adam.

But, you may ask, if Satan sinned, wasn't death the obvious result? Yes. Death for him. The Devil would have instantly experienced a spiritual death, a separation in his relationship with God. But there is nothing that points to his fall causing immediate cosmic consequences. He was not designed as titular head of the created order. It was Adam who made to rule and have dominion in the world. Not Satan. That is why it was Adam's sin that thrust all of nature into a maelstrom of death and destruction.

So for the theistic evolutionist who claims to believe in the Christian faith and accept the theological truths of the Scripture, there is a real problem indeed. How do we account for natural evil and death, present in all creation? To me this seems to be an insurmountable obstacle.

Essay 17
Have We Lost Our Souls?

Years ago I remember reading a science fiction short story about the depletion of the stock of human souls. I can't remember the author or the title… I wish I could. But I do remember that the gist of the story was that God (or fate or nature or whatever) had only created a certain number of souls. As the population of the earth grew to the abundance we see today, the quantity of available souls was completely reached. Doctors and midwives, parents and childcare workers, all began to notice that they were seeing children who were alive, but had only a vacant stare and no intellectual response. They seemed happy, in a sort of mindless bliss, but were missing the vital component that would make them fully human. What was missing? They had no souls. The reservoir of souls had all been used up. According to the story, the world had reached a stage where all beings genetically identifiable as *Homo sapiens* were only soulless human-appearing creatures. We had come to the end of humanity as true human beings.

This story came to mind today because I have been pondering C. S. Lewis's critically important book *The Abolition of Man*. At Advancing Native Missions we currently have four interns working in the office. As part of their program, they are reading this Lewis work. George Ainsworth, an ANM staff member, is leading them in their study. Knowing my devotion to Lewis, George asked if I wanted to join their discussion. I jumped at the chance. Thus prompted by this opportunity, I have reread *The Abolition of Man* for the first time in many years. What a book! Some believe that this may be Lewis's most important work. It certainly deserves attention as an amazingly prescient writing.

In this book Lewis takes to task a grammar book which he calls *The Green Book*. Beyond just discussing grammar, the authors of *The Green Book* were attempting to change students themselves. As Lewis observed, the authors were clearly redefining not only the use of language but values and fundamental beliefs. Basically they rejected the objective nature of truth and the idea of universal absolutes and mores. Lewis rightly asserts that these matters (call them first principles, natural law, human conscience, or just plain ol' right and wrong) are foundational in all of Western philosophy and civilization. We built our culture upon them. To abandon these building blocks of our society has tremendous consequences not only for the individual students who read this work, but for society as a whole.

In the 1940's, when Lewis wrote his book, he was seeing the beginnings of this move to jettison such fundamentals. The idea of a postmodern culture was still decades in the future. Now, what Lewis saw in a nascent form, we see full grown and endemic in our society. We are daily witnessing what Lewis "prophetically" saw in 1943.

One of the main points of *The Abolition of Man* is that by rejecting natural law, what Lewis calls the Tao, the natural way of things, we are rejecting what makes us truly human. When we remove first principles, absolute truth, we reduce man to something less than human. We create what Lewis calls "men without chests." By this he means there is a disconnect between our intellect and our passions. And without the mediating human factor, we become either thinking mechanisms or brute beasts.

For example, we may have intellects, thinking minds, but without a proper spiritual basis as responsible beings created in God's image, we are simply organic machines. Thinking is reduced to electrical pulses between synapses in our brains—nothing more. We are only fleshly computers. This is the position asserted by Francis Crick in his final major work, *The Astounding Hypothesis*. Crick was co-discoverer with James Watson of the structure of the DNA. For this he was awarded a Nobel Prize. However, with all his intelligence, Crick rejected the idea that we possess souls, something external to our material physiology. For him, our minds are only physical realities. The mind consists of nothing beyond electrical and chemical processes. We are organic super-computers, if you will. This is the same position held by many in our culture today.

At the other end of the spectrum we may be "men without chests" who are ruled by our physical urges. We are slaves to our passions, those barking dogs in the lower recesses of our psyches that Dostoyevsky wrote about. What is a human being? According to this perspective, we are only animals dominated by instinct, feelings and hormonal desires. There are no moral absolutes, no certainty in ethical matters. What is right is what I want to be right. Generally, the attitude is more like this: What is right is what I enjoy, what gives me pleasure. Humans are nothing but evolved, reasoning primates. We are not made a "little lower than the angels." Instead, we are only one step above gorillas.

The point is this: It is not our intelligence that makes us human. Nor is it our physical form. It is what is found in our chests—our values, our beliefs, our spiritual nature. What makes us human is our soul. And the evidence of our soulish nature is seen in the reality of natural law (absolutes, first principles, conscience). If we deny the existence of natural law, we deny what makes us truly human. To deny what fills our "chests," to dismiss the existence of the soul, is to reject the very essence of what it means to be a human being. We abolish mankind en masse.

Think this too far-fetched? Then consider the modern world. How do you explain gross immorality being promoted as simply "alternative life-styles"? How do you understand all the crime, violence, war, hatred, and terror of contemporary life? How do you deal with the slaughter of untold millions of unborn babies? Every year over 800,000 teens become pregnant out of wedlock in this country. Why is this happening? We kill each other over drugs, the very drugs that we use as an escape from the tedium and pain of life itself. Religious faith has become either something to be mocked or an excuse to justify our immoral behavior. God is ignored, or blamed for the mess we have created. In other words, the world is totally fouled up. And we have made it so. What we are experiencing is a society of "men without chests."

Essay 18
Raindrops Keep Falling on Our Heads

One of the premier events for Christian young people in this country is the Urbana conference. This event is sponsored by Intervarsity Christian ministries and is held every three years. It is one of the largest Christian youth events in the world. The most recent conference was December 27-31, 2015 and was held in St. Louis, MO. Advancing Native Missions (ANM) had a display there, with a number of staff representing ANM.

Back in our offices in Virginia, we received regular reports about what was happening at the conference. One of these reports noted that comments on social media from the conference were very interesting. There were a number of posts to Facebook and Twitter commenting on the fact that the LGBT community was not represented at the conference. Fascinating. Would you really expect the Lesbian-Gay-Bisexual-Transgender community to be a part of this conference? For some, apparently yes.

The first question that comes to mind is this: Who was posting these comments? They could have been members of the LGBT movement seeking to make their presence known at Urbana. They may have been posted by non-Christians attending the event. (There were over 600 decisions for Christ recorded at the conference.) Both of these groups could, and may have, accounted for some of the posts. However, I think it likely that many simply came from well-intentioned but rather naïve Christian believers. I know from speaking at youth events and to teen groups that many youthful Christians today do not hold the same views about homosexuality that is taught in the Bible. They question whether there is anything wrong with an "alternative sexual orientation." This is, sad to say, not uncommon today.

So the second question is: How did we get to this place? How did we get to the place where Christians, young or old, do not accept a clearly stated moral position plainly taught in the Bible? The answer is this: We got to this place a little bit at a time.

I am old enough to remember when the common view of homosexuality was completely different than it is today. It was viewed as abnormal, a perversion. It could be laughable (cf. Klinger on *M*A*S*H*). It was considered a mental illness by the medical community—even officially listed as such in the DSM (Diagnostic and Statistical Manual of Mental Disorders—not being removed from the DSM until 1973). And homosexuality was definitely considered a sin. The Christian community was certain about that—because the Bible plainly stated this. So what happened?

This is what happened. Those in the homosexual community, and their allies in Hollywood and the media, launched an effort to convert the thinking of mainstream America. It started slowly. Then it grew.

Essay 18: *Raindrops Keep Falling on Our Heads*

As I recall, one of first characters that was presented as gay on TV was a semi-regular purse snatcher on *Barney Miller*, a program back in the '70's. The show also sometimes featured a gay police officer, who desperately tried to stay under the radar regarding his sexual orientation. From such small beginnings, the snowball started down the hill. It grew and picked up momentum. Talk shows got on board. Comedians took up the effort. Sitcoms such as *Will and Grace* made gays main characters. Now, it is hard to find a TV show that doesn't have at least one homosexual character. Today the snowball is huge. Its presence fills our TV screens.

Along with the increased presence of gay and lesbians in the media, the propaganda came. "We are a minority, suffering discrimination," we heard. "Give us equal rights!" was proclaimed. Rainbow flags abounded and pink triangles became badges of honor. Before long, to say anything negative about homosexuality was hate speech. And to say that it is morally wrong is not only offensive, it is un-American, even un-Christian.

And so we arrive at the place where Christian young people cannot understand why the LGBT community is not represented at a Christian conference.

There is a principle at work here. I call it "The Raindrop Principle." Let me explain. How do you get wet in a rain storm? One drop at a time. There may be many drops falling at once. But there are still only individual drops hitting you one at time. And if you get hit by enough single drops you are soon soaking wet.

How did our thinking about homosexuality change in this country? One drop at a time. One image. One slogan on a bumper sticker. One TV character. One joke on a talk show. One political speech. One film promoting the LGBT agenda. Incremental and consistent exposure to a certain idea, a certain view, slowly affected the minds and hearts of Americans, and our entire mindset about homosexuality was transformed.

Homosexuality is not the only example of the Raindrop Principle evident in 21st century America. There are many. We used to think that having a child out of wedlock was not only a sin, it was shameful. Now it is common, and commonly accepted. Living together without being married? Never! Yet now it is not just common, it has become the norm. Christianity was once viewed as the true religion. Now all religions are basically the same. It was once believed that Jesus was THE Savior, the only way to God. Now, Jesus is but one of many ways; all faiths are paths to God. And truth itself… there was a day when we knew (rightly) that some things are true and others are false. But now truth is up for grabs. There is no absolute truth… so it is generally said.

The point is this: You cannot be too careful about what you allow into your mind. We live in a media culture where our minds are bombarded with images, facts, concepts, data, theories, and ideas constantly. Some of these are true. Some are consistent with a Christian worldview. Many, probably most, are not—not at all. We must learn to filter what comes into our minds. Each one of these things is a drop, just one drop. But if enough drops enter our minds (and our hearts) we will end up soaking wet. In other words, we will have been transformed, and probably not realize that any change has taken place. Indeed, we probably did not even know it was raining.

Essay 19
Alchemy in the Academy

Something dangerous and scary is probably occurring right now at a university or college near you. It may be disguised as a seminar on wellness, a class on well-being, or a conference on integrative health. You might find it listed in the college catalog in courses labeled "Mindfulness Training" or "Contemplative Learning." It could more blatantly be offered as a program for student/faculty that utilizes yoga, Tai Chi, or meditation as an aid to mental and physical health. And usually somewhere in the literature for this seminar, class or program you will find references to the "wealth" of scientific evidence that proves that mindfulness (or yoga, or contemplation, or whatever) is proven to be the panacea for all ills in body and soul.

In our local environment (I live in central Virginia), we have our local manifestation of this trend. It is called the Contemplative Sciences Center (CSC). This is a heavily funded initiative at the University of Virginia. The funding comes from UVA alumni who have pumped millions of dollars into the CSC with the intent of making yoga, mindfulness and other "contemplative sciences" available to the entire staff, faculty, and students of UVA. Their goal is to integrate contemplative practices in all the various colleges of the University, and for yoga and meditation to become part of the everyday life at UVA. Beginning only in 2012, they have (unfortunately) thus far been very successful.

It is disturbing for Eastern religion to be promoted in a state-funded school of higher learning. (What a wonderful example of our tax dollars at work!) It is frustrating that Hindu and Buddhist beliefs and practices are allowed free rein in our schools, yet if we dare pray in Jesus's name it is considered "un-American" and anti-Constitutional. Yes, all this is greatly upsetting. And there are many things we could say about how disconcerting this is. But there is one aspect to this whole "mess" that I want to consider today. It is the pseudo-scientific patina glowing on the surface of the whole phenomenon.

For the past 150 years or so academia in America has been largely secular, mainly given over to materialistic naturalism. Long ago we left our Judeo-Christian roots, and consequently abandoned belief in the supernatural. Science and naturalism reigned supreme in most of the hallowed halls of our universities and colleges. But naturalism and rationalism have been in many circles swept away by our postmodern rejection of all absolutes, including rationalistic absolutes. Nothing is certain. No truth is absolute. So we question everything. And as a result we have reopened the door to the preternatural, the world of paranormal phenomena and spiritual occurrences. But while moving forward in this process, we have also been reluctant to aban-

Essay 19: *Alchemy in the Academy*

don our scientific roots. So, it has become necessary to find a scientific rationale to justify mystical practices and beliefs. For example, why practice yoga? Nowadays we don't do yoga because it will unite our individual souls with the World Soul, making us one with Brahman. No we practice yoga because it is healthy for mind and body; it lowers our blood pressure and boosts our immune system. And we have the scientific studies to prove it. (So it is said.)

What we are now experiencing is a weird amalgamation of science and the supernatural. In a real way, we have returned to the magical beliefs and experimental sorcery of the late Middle Ages and the Renaissance. Our scientists talk like sorcerers, and our religious gurus use the jargon of science. Subtly and slowly, yet inexorably, over the past few decades we have returned to the world of Paracelsus and Cornelius Agrippa. We are like Isaac Newton, propounding scientific theories by day and practicing alchemy by night. We are modern-day scholastic magicians.

In my ministry, I address the subject of the occult quite a bit. The growing presence of occult belief and practice in our culture is one of my greatest concerns. Concomitant with this is the increasing presence of eastern mysticism in our society. This is not surprising—both worldviews are very similar. This growing presence is an alarming trend. And what makes it even more alarming is that metaphysical principles and concepts are being packaged in a way that makes them seem scientifically valid and acceptable. I believe it is this mixture of science and the supernatural that is especially perilous for our culture. Ever try to talk to people living in this particular world? It is hard to argue against supernatural experience that is supposedly substantiated by scientific theory.

This trend pops up all over the place. Books such as *The Tao of Physics* by Fritjof Capra and *The Dancing Wu Li Masters* by Gary Zukav assert that modern physics and the theories of quantum mechanics have definite parallels in Hindu and Buddhist beliefs. ESP and the paranormal have been studied as scientific disciplines in universities like Duke and UVA for the past 80 years or so. Grant money is being expended so university professors can study children who purportedly have memories of past lives. Reincarnation has become science! And now the benefits of meditation, yoga and mindfulness are considered medically verifiable. Indeed, they have become required disciplines in many schools for the health sciences.

Insight on this situation can be found in the writings of C. S. Lewis. Lewis was an amazing writer. So much of what is occurring in western culture today was foreseen by this prescient author. *The Abolition of Man* deals with the shift in worldviews that Lewis saw happening in the educational field of the 1940's. Lewis further expounded on these matters in the final volume of his fictional Space Trilogy, *That Hideous Strength*. This work is virtually prophetic. I won't take time to discuss the plot of this book. I suggest you read it for yourself. However, I mention *That Hideous Strength* because it paints a picture of the horrific threat to be found in the mixture of science and the supernatural. When academics and scientists begin toying with the paranormal, they are getting more than they bargained for. They do not realize that there are genuine spiritual entities behind the phenomena they are studying and promoting. Yes, as Medieval as it may sound to some, there are demons and they are active in the world today. They are the actual forces behind ESP, mystical experiences and supernatural events. What this means is that we are opening our schools, our homes, our minds to the devilish in the guise of the scientific and the scholarly.

Lewis also points out that this could not have happened in the early 19th century. Back then, naturalistic scholars were true materialists. Yet they still believed in truth, and that it was discoverable. They also still functioned within a moral framework, a Judeo-Christian consensus in society, although they may have rejected its particulars. They were a different breed from the scientists and academics of our day. Today we tend to be more postmodern. There are no absolutes. Everything is relative and existential. So we are open to any possibility—whether scientific or preternatural. Elements and elementals, algorithms and alchemy—all are acceptable, all are possible.

Lewis commented in *That Hideous Strength* on the moral and intellectual decay of society, and the resulting equal acceptance of both science and magic. Lewis asserts in such a climate Man comes to the point that he thinks he can transcend nature, and become his own god. Whether through science or witchcraft, Man can do anything. Lewis says this: "What should they find incredible, since they believed no longer in a rational universe? What should they regard as too obscene, since they held that all morality was a mere subjective by-product of the physical and economic situation of men? The time was ripe. From the point of view which is accepted in Hell, the whole history of our earth had led up this moment. There was now at last a real chance for fallen Man to shake off that limitation of his powers which mercy had imposed upon him as a protection from the full results of his fall. If this succeeded, Hell would be at last incarnate."

God help us! We may be living in the day when we are seeing Hell incarnate. And there are (ironically enough) twin agents involved in the birth to this spiritual monster. Magic is the mother, and Science is the midwife.

Essay 20
The Master Artist

A fascinating book to read and ponder is *The Rage Against God* by Peter Hitchens. Peter Hitchens is the brother of the late Christopher Hitchens, a noted journalist and outspoken atheist. In this book Hitchens describes his journey to faith in Christ from a background in staunch atheism. As the title indicates, he also deals with the anger so many atheists exhibit against God and religion. He makes an interesting point. Why are the atheists so angry? If we believe in God, and they don't, so be it. Why not just let each person have his own beliefs? Why be so enraged about the whole thing?

If you read atheist literature, websites, and the like, you will see this anger very prominently. And one of the main things that really ticks them off is the presence of evil, suffering and wrong in the world. They raise this objection constantly: If God exists, and He is good, why does He allow so much suffering in the world? Good question. Indeed, it is probably one of the most frequently asked questions that I come across. For many people the idea of a good God and an evil world seem incompatible. Why are things this way?

We have dealt with this question in another essay, "Why Does God Allow Evil?" You can check that out to get some insight on the question. However, in this essay I would like to take a stab at this topic again.

One thing that helps me deal with this issue is developing a clearer understanding of God, and seeing a bigger picture of who He is. I accept as a basic proposition that God is good (Psalm 25:1, 34:8, 100:5, Lamentations 3:25, 1Peter 2:3). To do good is basic to His nature. And what He does is good. So when He created mankind with free will, and a world in which evil could possibly exist as a result of free will, then that was a good thing. He cannot do otherwise. Evil was not his original intent, nor His desire for the world He made. But He allowed it because His love necessitated that we exist as free moral agents, with true choice.

Further, understanding God's goodness, along with His wisdom and omnipotence, also helps me to accept that God is able to take even the most evil thing and incorporate it into His sovereign (and good) plan for mankind. He didn't ordain evil. But He can use it. He doesn't approve of sin. But He can turn it to good. He doesn't like to see His children suffer. But He is big enough and wise enough to transform even our pain into something glorious (cf. Romans 8:18, 2 Corinthians 4:18). As Rick Warren says, "God never wastes a hurt." That is how wonderfully great, wise and powerful our Lord truly is.

Let me illustrate by using an analogy. Of course, as with any analogy, there are limitations to how useful this is. And it can only give a brief glimpse into a larger reality. But maybe it will help us to understand a little bit about both His sovereignty and His goodness.

Essay 20: *The Master Artist*

Imagine a great painter, someone on par with a Raphael or a Da Vinci. He is a true master of his art. He can do things with a brush that awe and inspire anyone who sees his work. His works have deservedly earned him worldwide fame.

Now imagine the painter in his studio working on his latest painting. His hope is that when finished this work will be his greatest triumph. It will truly be his magnum opus. The painter has a vision for a true masterpiece that will exceed anything he has done before. As he works, he can see with his mind's eye the awesome beauty of the finished painting. It is with joy and anticipation that he carefully places each brushstroke on the canvas.

After working many hours, he decides to take a break. He leaves the studio for a bit. While he is gone, his very young son creeps into the studio. He creeps because he has been repeatedly told not to enter here without an adult being with him. He has also been warned not to play with his father's paints and the brushes. The child shyly approaches the unfinished masterpiece. Young though he is, he admires his father, and wants to be like him. So he decides to assume his father's role and try his hand at painting. He grabs a brush and plunges it into the paint on his father's palette. With a gleam in his eye he liberally creates streaks of color across his father's work. Again and again he loads the brush in order to daub and smear the painting with his own creative efforts. And he is very pleased with his work. To him it is beautiful. He cannot comprehend the ugliness of what he has done.

What do you think will happen when the painter returns? Will he be justly angered? Certainly. Will he be upset with what his own son has done? Yes. Does he now hate his child? Of course not. He loves him, even though the son has apparently ruined a master work.

After dealing appropriately with his son, the father returns to gaze at his deformed painting. What does he do now? Does he try to scrape away all the paint the child smeared on the canvas? But that would only make things worse. Does he destroy the painting? Start over? The painter decides he will do none of these things. Being a master artist, a true maestro in his craft, the painter decides that instead of destroying what his son has done he will actually use it. He will incorporate the streaks and smears and splotches that are his son's handiwork and make them a part of his masterpiece. This will mean altering his original vision for the painting. But he now visualizes a new master work that will still be beautiful.

And so he works. Some of the paint the child applied to the canvas is still wet. The master artist adds color to this in some places. In other places he changes, molds and transforms it. What was unattractive and unpleasant is now part of his new vision. In some places, the paint has dried. So the artist works around it, or paints over it, or comes up with a creative touch near it. He does this in such a way that the ugly smudges of the child's wayward efforts are now a beautiful portion of the overall work. Indeed, in some places what the artist had painted earlier now has a fresh look—an even more glorious appearance—and all because of their contrast with the sections of the painting the child messed up. The painter is able to transform the child's work into something good and beautiful.

Does this mean that what his son did was okay? No. What the child did was not good. It was ugly. It was done in rebellious disobedience. It is not what the father/painter initially planned or desired. But the master painter, being the great artist that he is, was able to take the errors and wrongs of his child and turn them into something good. The artist was still able to create a true masterpiece, despite the harm done by the son.

Child of God, please understand that though this is only a feeble portrayal of what our heavenly Father does, it does illustrate in some small measure a genuine truth. Evil is real. Sin is bad. Suffering is real, and horrible. And God abhors all these. But He is so powerful, wise, creative and capable that He can take anything, even sin, even evil, and make something good come out of it. For the child of God, Romans 8:28 is still true. And one day we will see the ultimate fulfillment of this verse in all its majesty and glory.

So what do we do when we are in pain, when we suffer, when evil is shouting its presence in our lives? One thing we can do is remember our Lord and Father, the Heavenly Artist, is creating a masterpiece out of our lives. We need to see the bigger picture. This is what God always does in the lives of His children.

Essay 21
Why Doesn't God Destroy Evil?

Do you ever read anything written by atheists, skeptics and those who actively oppose Christianity? I do. And one of the most common arguments they use against our faith is the existence of evil. They say if God is truly good and really all powerful, why doesn't He just do away with evil? Why doesn't He just wipe it off the earth, completely eradicate it? God must not exist, because if He did, then evil would not be allowed to exist. That's what they say.

So...what about it? What do you think? Should God just sovereignly, completely and immediately rid the world of all evil? BLAM! By divine decree all sin, crime, violence, war, abuse, and wrongdoing are done away with. They're gone.

Seems like a good idea, doesn't it? It seems like a pretty nifty solution. Well, at least at first glance. But there are some real problems with this approach. Let's consider a few things.

First of all, God is all-knowing and all-wise. He sees all things. And because God sees all things, He knows all things. And in His sovereign wisdom (and grace) He sees how He can use anything/everything to accomplish His plans and purposes. He can even turn evil into something that ultimately results in good. It doesn't mean that evil is not truly evil. But He is big enough and wise enough to convert even wrong into something with good results. Indeed, God often uses evil things to actually benefit us, to help us to grow, and to advance His kingdom. Have you ever learned from being mistreated, suffering, going through pain or hardship? Often hardship, evils in our lives, are training tools in the hands of God.

There is a second consideration. Suppose God were to just get rid of evil? The "BLAM" I mentioned earlier. He just speaks, and evil ceases to exist at all. Now think about this. God is holy and righteous. As an absolutely just and perfect Being, if He acted simply in His righteousness and justice without exercising His mercy, He would have to do eradicate evil completely. He would have to get rid of all evil. His holiness would demand a complete job. He could not do it halfway. Without His mercy in place, the justice of God (in this proposed scenario) would do away with all evil at one "whack." But moral evil is not detached from human beings. WE are the ones who commit evil deeds, have evil thoughts, exhibit evil intent. To rid the world of evil would mean that God would have to get rid of evil people. Let me ask you... have you ever lied? Stolen? Cheated? Been unkind? Been selfish? Treated someone meanly? Have you ever done evil? If God were to eradicate all evil right now, He would have to get rid of every human being. Every one of us. Not just the leaders of ISIS or Kim Jong Un. Not just the Hitlers and Jack the

Essay 21: *Why Doesn't God Destroy Evil?*

Rippers, but also the Mother Teresas and Billy Grahams. Everyone! You would not be here anymore—neither would I! We should remember that Lamentations 3:22 says that it is because of His "mercies that we are not consumed." Good point.

One final thought, because God sees the big picture He also sees what will happen with evil individuals in the future. He knows the futures of every individual on earth. Perhaps one reason He shouldn't just get rid of evil people is that He sees what is going to happen to those people in the future. You see, God is still in the life-transforming business. He still takes evil people—terrorists, murderers, thieves, rapists, drug addicts, drug dealers, wife-beaters and child molesters—and turns these individuals into Christians, children of God, good men and women. He changes hearts and redirects lives. I know. I have seen Him do it.

Think about it...

Persecution is an evil. But if God just did away with persecution, with persecutors.... There would never have been an Apostle Paul.

Suppose God prohibited all human-trafficking and all slavery... then he would have had to destroy all traffickers and slave traders... and there would never have been a John Newton, and we would not have "Amazing Grace."

Is Islam an evil system? Definitely. Does God hate evil? Certainly. But supposed God removed from the earth of all mullahs and imams, all Sharia jurists, all defenders of Islam, all jihadists... then He would have had to destroy many great men of God before they ever came to know Him. At Advancing Native Missions we are privileged to work with indigenous missionaries who came from Muslim backgrounds. Some were trained as imams. Some were experts in Sharia law. Some were violent fighters for Islam, even belonging to terrorist organizations. But now? Now through God's grace and the transforming power of the Gospel they are firebrands for the Kingdom of God. This would not be the case if many years back God had just wiped out all violent and wicked followers of Islam.

Is violence, fighting, drug dealing, and gang warfare evil? Certainly. But if God did away with all gang members and all drug addicts... then we at Advancing Native Missions would never have had the privilege of knowing a man like David Yone Mo. David was a very wicked man. Yet God delivered him from gangs and crime and drugs. God turned him into a powerful minister of the Gospel. Through David's ministry, Myanmar Young Crusaders, tens of thousands of people have come to Christ. Through his work many hundreds of drug addicts have been delivered and become productive citizens. There are so many children—orphans, abandoned children, children of lepers—who have been fed, educated, and discipled because of David. David has gone home to be with the Lord Jesus now. But he has left behind a powerful Christian legacy—that would never have come into existence if God had simply erased all drug addicts and gang leaders off the earth.

Do you understand? God allows evil to exist because the only way to get rid of moral evil is to get rid of evil people. Therefore, God allows evil to exist because He is merciful! In addition, God allows evil to exist because as wicked, hurtful and bad as it all is, the Lord is mighty enough to work greater things out of the wrongs of this world, including evil itself. God does not approve of sin, nor does He cause it. But He can turn it to good, for His glory and the benefit of people.

P.S. Consider the following Scriptures regarding this issue: Genesis 50:18-20, Romans 8:28, Isaiah 46:9-10, Ephesians 1:11, Romans 9:22-23. Also, if you would like to read the story of David Yone Mo, it is found in a book entitled *Never Say Die* by Doug Hsu. You can purchase this book from Advancing Native Missions.

Essay 22
Peace at All Costs?

I am a history buff. Always have been. I am also one of those people who is fascinated by dates and what happened on certain days. For example, I am writing this on Friday, March 18, 2016. On this date in history in the year A.D. 37 the Roman Senate proclaimed Caligula as Emperor. (Something they would come to regret!) In 978 King Edward of England was murdered, joining thousands of other Christian martyrs in the roll call of faith. In 1852 the Wells Fargo Company was founded. In 1922 Mohandas Gandhi was sentenced to six years in prison for civil disobedience. In 1961 the Pillsbury Dough Boy made his debut.

Also on this date, Neville Chamberlain was born in 1869. Do you remember Chamberlain? He was the Prime Minister of Great Britain from 1937 to 1940. Chamberlain is best known for his attempts to keep the peace, and avoid war with Germany. As the

1930's progressed, Hitler became increasingly aggressive in his plans to dominate Europe. Chamberlain met with Hitler in a series of conferences in 1938. He returned from Germany in September with the Munich Accord. Chamberlain apparently believed that he had corralled Hitler, and that *Der Führer's* expansionist effort was at an end. Indeed, he had Hitler's assurances as to this fact. Chamberlain famously reported, "I have returned from Germany with peace for our time." That peace was very short-lived, however. Within a year Britain would be at war with Germany, and World War II would have begun.

Historians debate about Chamberlain and his tenure as Prime Minister. Was the Munich Accord he signed with Hitler an effective strategic measure, or a bumbling mistake of truly historic proportions? The jury is still out. However, my (limited) study of Chamberlain leaves with me with one impression—he was basically clueless in understanding Hitler and his intentions. He wanted to think the best of Herr Hitler and optimistically hope that everyone would just "play nice" and get along. He was really a man out of touch with the times.

Chamberlain was probably a good man, a good patriot, and in some ways an effective administrator. But his failure to accurately assess Hitler and the Nazi regime was disastrous. Can I tell you something? We live in a world of Neville Chamberlains. This is especially true in the church. When it comes to what is happening in our world, most Christians just want everyone to "play nice and get along." It doesn't matter that our Enemy is out to destroy us, and he is launching an all-out assault on our morals, our doctrine, and our ability to influence our culture. It doesn't matter that we coddle sinners and hold up wicked people as heroes. It doesn't matter that we compromise biblical truth, and glory in our "tolerance" and "open-mindedness." These things don't matter. We want to live in a "nice" world where peace reigns, and everybody gets along just fine.

Essay 22: *Peace at All Costs?*

This is the world we live in today. A world where the ugliness of sin is no longer recognized. Good is now evil, and wrong is now right. And if you think differently... if you attempt to point out a biblical view of morals and truth... then you are old-fashioned, narrow-minded, and (above all) legalistic. Shame on you for being so judgmental. What is wrong with you? Why can't you just "love" everybody and accept everyone just the way they are?

Too many people say these very things. And what they are actually revealing about themselves is that they are clueless about what is really happening in our world. There is no peace for us. We are at war! We are already in a war where the Enemy is expanding his territory and, sadly, we are naively allowing him to do it. We should be girding ourselves for battle, and raising the banner of righteousness, justice, truth, and virtue. Instead we declare "peace for our time" and let the Enemy roll right over us. God help us! (If He doesn't, we are doomed.) God give us men like those in ancient Issachar, who understood the times they lived in and knew what the children of God should do (1 Chronicles 12:32). We need to stand for God's truth and God's way. We need to be warriors for the Gospel, "fighting the good fight of faith" (1 Timothy 6:12). We need to heed the words of Martin Luther, "Peace if possible, truth at all costs." We need to once again "Stand up, stand up for Jesus!"

Essay 23
An Existential View of Evil

We live in a day when everything is relative. According to the popular mythology, nothing is absolute. (How popular mythologists get by with this one absolute I will never understand.) Truth and morality are situational, personal, relational and relative. The all-too common thinking runs something like this: "If I think it is okay, then it is okay. If I perceive it as moral and good, then it must be moral and good." Usually what such thinkers actually mean is "if what I am doing is something I want to do—that makes me happy—then it must be good."

This approach is completely out of sync with a biblical worldview—where there are absolutes, and some things are just plain right, and some things are just plain wrong. Unfortunately this mythology has even crept into the church. One way this relativistic view of morality shows up, oddly enough, is in how Christians define sin and evil. Let me illustrate with a few examples.

Some of you may remember what happened in Augusta County, VA in December of 2015. Students in a local public school were asked to copy Arabic calligraphy, which happened to be the Shahadah. The Shahadah is the basic faith affirmation of Islam—"There is no God but Allah, and Muhammad is his prophet." The students were told that this was the Shahadah, but they were not given a translation. It was stated that this was the basic Islamic "statement of faith." Parents saw this assignment and were outraged. Rapidly voices of protest were heard. So many parents objected that school officials actually ordered all the schools in the county closed. Many people thought the parents' objections were a bit extreme. What was the big deal? The Arabic was not translated. Students would not necessarily know what the text said. And they were not being asked to accept the Shahadah, to convert to Islam. What was so wrong?

Let me offer another example. Yoga is extremely popular. It seems like every other commercial on TV has someone doing yoga. (Although what yoga has to do with selling cars, laundry detergent or insurance is an interesting question.) You can take yoga classes at the local YMCA, health club or even in churches. Since we are very health conscious society, many people are curious about yoga. I am often asked by Christians whether they should practice yoga. I always try to discourage people from doing yoga because it is firmly rooted in Hindu belief and practice. The very word yoga is Sanskrit and means "yoke" or "union." The entire purpose of yoga is to unite the individual soul with the World Soul, or Brahman, the impersonal ultimate "god" of Hinduism. In addition, each of the *asanas*, or poses of Hatha Yoga has reference to some Hindu god or belief. For example, the Lord of the Dance pose refers to Shiva. The Eagle *asana* represents Garuda, the eagle god associated with Vishnu. And the list goes on and on. However, several times I have had Christian say that because they do not believe in the Hindu gods, or the spiritual goals of yoga, that it is okay for them to do it. After all, they are only doing it for the physical exercise, not as a spiritual discipline. It's okay, as long as you don't personally believe in the spiritual aspects of it. So there was nothing to worry about. Makes sense, right?

One more example will suffice. A few years ago I was teaching on how prevalent the occult has become in our culture. I was explaining that we tend to not take the occult very seriously. For example, kids conduct séances at parties, just for fun. Ouija boards are considered games—even being sold by Parker Brothers. However, despite the light-hearted approach to such things, they are actually very serious. Indeed, God condemns all forms of witchcraft, fortunetelling and occult practice in no uncertain terms (e.g., Deuteronomy 18:14-19). I also explained that any involvement in the occult was serious, and should be confessed as sin. One lady in the class, a very devout Christian, spoke up. She admitted that as a youth she had been in a séance, and had played with Ouija boards. But she saw no problem with this, because she did not take it seriously. Because she did not believe in these things, there was really nothing wrong with it. There was nothing to confess. Makes sense, doesn't it?

Were the Christians who dismissed the matter of the Shahadah being used in public schools right? It was no big deal, right? Was this mother correct, that false gods are not real gods so there is nothing wrong with her child coloring symbols of these gods? And if you do not believe in Ouija boards or séances, then what is wrong with having a little fun with them? No harm, no foul—right?

Wrong! First of all, these things are strictly prohibited by God in the Scriptures. How can we not take seriously something that God condemns as wicked and sinful? It is no light matter to dismiss God's revelation on these matters. What God says is sin, is sin indeed.

Secondly, as already noted, we don't take false religion, idolatry and witchcraft (the occult) nearly seriously enough in America today. We don't see them as God sees them. He takes them very seriously. Indeed, in ancient Israel, involvement in idolatry or the occult was a capital offense. Yes, you could be executed for practicing these things. Such things are truly grave matters.

But there is another concern here. In each of these three examples, the rationale for dismissing the seriousness of issue was that each individual did not have a commitment of personal belief or acceptance of the specific matter under consideration. The students were not asked to believe the Shahadah. The child did understand the meaning of mandalas, and thus did not believe in their power. The Christian lady did not believe in séances or Ouija boards, so her involvement was innocent. Do you notice a common approach to these matters? The rightness or wrongness of the action is based on personal experience. Something is only truly wrong if you have a personal belief in its reality. If you do not believe in it, then practicing it cannot be truly wrong. Its morality (or lack thereof) is based on the person and his/her belief or disbelief in its reality. In other words, morality (or immorality) is an existential experience.

These examples illustrate what is happening in our culture. Our problem here is that we have made morality a personal, relative, existential experience. We have rejected morality as an objective absolute. Something is not wrong because it is just wrong. It is not even wrong if God says it is wrong. It is only wrong if I believe it is wrong.

But from a biblical perspective, morality is not subjective. It is a matter of an absolute nature, ordained by God. Let me emphasize this point by changing our three illustrations into parallel situations. Let's see if this existential, subjective approach still fits.

Essay 23: *An Existential View of Evil*

Suppose that instead of being asked to copy the Shahadah in Arabic, the students had been asked to copy a text in another language, say in Hebrew or Latin. And suppose, though untranslated, the text was from a Medieval grimoire, a book of magical incantations. Now suppose the text was actually a prayer to Lucifer, invoking Satan as a great and powerful god and pledging allegiance to him and his kingdom of darkness. Would this be objectionable?

As for my second example, suppose instead of Hindu gods the various yoga poses referred to demons. Would it be okay to do the Satan pose, or the Lucifer *asana*, or the Beelzebub posture? A Christian could execute such a pose in complete ignorance. But would you knowingly do an exercise that represents the Devil and is designed to honor him? And if it was pointed out to you that each pose was intended not only to represent demons, but to conjure them and their power—would you still want to do yoga?

Now for the third example, let's be a little extreme. Suppose this fine Christian lady admitted that she had cheated on her husband and had had an adulterous affair. But she excused this by saying that it was just in fun. She didn't love the guy, or make any kind of commitment to him. In fact, she did not really believe in adultery. She believed in committed monogamy. So her behavior was not sinful, and no confession was necessary because she did not believe in the reality of what she had done. Would this be reasonable? Or does it sound foolish?

You see the problem we are facing? We have made morality a matter of personal choice. Even Christians do this. No, we don't (usually) take this position when it comes to obvious sins (murder, adultery, thievery, etc.), but other sins are a different matter. Especially if it is something we enjoy and find fun. But that is not God's view. What he says is sin is sin indeed. And witchcraft, idolatry and honoring false gods are wrong because they are just plain wrong.

That's it. God says what is right and what is wrong, and that is the way it is. End of story.

The truth is this—some things are intrinsically evil and immoral. It doesn't matter if we believe them to be so, or not. They are wrong just because they are wrong, evil things in their own right. It is not wrong because of our acceptance or rejection of them. They are wrong because they are wrong by their very nature. Arabic proclamations of Allah being the true god, activities sacred to false gods, and occult practices from the kingdom of darkness are wrong in and of themselves. That's all there is to it.

Bottom Line: Some things are just evil, plain and simple, and the Christian should have nothing to do with them. Period. And that's the absolute truth!

Essay 24
Reason—A Double-Edged Sword

In the 17th century, a giant intellect arose in France by the name of René Descartes. He is considered by many as the father of modern philosophy. His thinking certainly served as a harbinger for the period known as the Enlightenment that would follow in the next century.

Descartes was a son of the church. He did not set out to reject faith or deny church dogma. What he did purpose to do was explore with his mind the limits of human knowledge. His pursuit of knowledge is said to have begun with a series of three visions, which he believed were divine visitations. Following these heavenly encounters, he began to explore what could be known through reason alone. There is an apocryphal legend that says he enclosed himself in a barrel for these ruminations. Although this is a fanciful tale, he did seclude himself in order to explore the power of his own reason.

His thinking went along these lines. He would choose to get rid of all external authority. He would doubt everything, only keeping what his own reason indicated. Having jettisoned all authority, he was left with nothing but doubt. However, since he doubted, he reasoned that this indicated that he had thoughts, therefore he was a thinking creature. And if he could think, then he had existence—only something that is real, in existence, can think. This is the origin of his famous phrase—*cogito ergo sum*, "I think, therefore I am."

Based on the fact of his own existence as a thinking being, Descartes then began to mentally explore the limits of knowledge. You might imagine that doubting all externals and being confined within one's own mind, that there would not be much you could know. But according to Descartes, this is not the case. Using only his ability to think, he began to reason out the basic principles of mathematics, fundamental ideas of truth and morality, and even a proof for the existence of God. (This is a variation of the ontological proof for God's existence.) Later he recorded the results of his thinking. He went on to produce multiple works on mathematics, philosophy and theology.

As noted earlier, Descartes did not purpose to oppose the church. He considered himself a devout believer. He even wrote one work, *Meditations on First Philosophy*, as an apologetic for the church. However, his system of rejecting external and previous authorities in favor of pure reason had a profound impact on the philosophy and theology that followed after him. Christianity does not stand in contradiction to reason. However, our faith is based on an authority external to ourselves. We believe in a God who has revealed Himself to us in various ways, most notably in His Son and in the Scriptures. Descartes' approach opened the door to rationalism—to the idea that *only* what can be known through reason should be accepted. As a result, thinking individuals began to call into the question the authority of the Scriptures themselves. Questioning descended into denial and rejection. The Age of Reason was the result. Rationalism became the dominant philosophy of the Modern Age, and affected the disciplines of science, history, philosophy and religion. For many, Descartes' "barrel experience" sounded the death knell of biblical Christianity, and religion in general.

Ever wonder why many secular scientists, atheists and agnostics, and skeptical academicians are so vehemently opposed to religion in general, and to Christianity in particular? Why would men like Richard Dawkins proclaim that God is a delusion? Or Christopher Hitchens assert that God is not good? Directly or indirectly it can be traced back to Descartes.

Poor Descartes. I think he would be shocked and dismayed by what his mental exercises have brought about in the world. He never intended to upend faith and attack religion as being "unreasonable."

This is why I refer to reason as a double-edged sword. Reason and Christianity are not opposed to one another, and they are not mutually exclusive. Many of the greatest thinkers in human history, Descartes himself included, were men of faith. Indeed, I firmly believe that reason and Christianity go hand in hand. I also believe that the Christian faith is the most reasonable belief system in the world— despite the contrary claims of atheism, naturalism, scientism, or any other ism. But reason by itself, apart from the divine, may lead men away from God rather than to Him. Reason may cut both ways. It may lead us to a better understanding of the divine, or in the exact opposite direction, an outright rejection of God.

One other point needs to be made. While reason is a wonderful thing in itself, it is not the only thing. Descartes' mental journey sought to explore the limits of reason alone. However, reason alone cannot explain everything. Consider the limits of reasonable systems of knowledge. The ancient Ptolemaic system of cosmology is often ridiculed today. But it was based on observation, sophisticated calculations, and the available knowledge of the day. It was a reasonable system. But it was wrong. Newton's theories brought about a revolution in knowledge. They are soundly reasonable. Yet, many of his ideas were contradicted by Einstein's theories. So it goes. There may come a day when new discoveries overturn the ideas of Einstein. It is possible, maybe probable. Reason alone is not sufficient. Increased knowledge, and reasoning based on this knowledge, does give us a better understanding of the universe—but this can only go so far. There is another legitimate source of knowledge that gives us absolute certainty in what we know. This is found in the revelations given us by God, in His word and in His Son. This knowledge is certain, accurate and assured.

The bottom line is this: We thank God for our wonderful human mind. Our reason is an invaluable gift from our Creator. We should use it wisely, in His service. We are also thankful for our faith, which is truly a reasonable faith. Thus we are grateful for both reason and faith.

Essay 25
The Dangers of Subjectivism

Recently I have been doing research on the Emergent Church. Just in case you are not familiar with this movement, let me give you a little background. The Emergent Church movement originated in conversations between various pastors, youth pastors and church leaders back in the 1990's. They were concerned about certain trends and practices they saw in the church. They were especially concerned about how relevant and effective the church was in reaching a postmodern culture. Out of their conversations arose an entire movement which has swept through America, Britain, Australia and other parts of the world.

The original ambitions of those involved in these conversations were noble and good. However, in their efforts to address the concerns of a postmodern society, they ended up becoming a postmodern movement. It seems, at least in their thinking, that to be relevant you must accommodate yourself to the culture—even if this accommodation involves sacrificing some of the foundational truths of the Christian faith.

One of their accommodations involves the very nature of truth and knowledge itself. A hallmark of the Emergent Church is that is rejects objectivity. Indeed, they assert that there is no such thing as objective reality—whether you are talking about morals and ethics or theology and our knowledge of God. As Tony Jones, one of their leaders, has stated, "Emergents think objectivity is as real as unicorns." In usual postmodern fashion Emergents believe that all truth, knowledge, morality, theology, whatever is relative, uncertain, and completely subjective. For them, truth is discoverable through dialogue, relationships and experience. But there is nothing objective to discover—only the subjective existential reality of the moment.

This is a very dangerous position to hold. In fact, much more dangerous than it would appear at first glance. Let's take a moment and consider why I say this.

C.S. Lewis once wrote an essay on "The Poison of Subjectivism." Although written in 1943, this essay could be a contemporary commentary on our society, and postmodernism in particular. Lewis presciently makes many observations about the logical fallacies of subjectivism, and the inherent dangerous consequences of accepting this idea.

First of all, Lewis notes that to speak of subjectivism in morals is not only dangerous but unreasonable. For example, most people would certainly declare their intent to improve in moral behavior, whether individually or as a society. Our desire is to do better, to grow in goodness as people. Yet, how are we to judge improvement? If there is no external, objective standard or morality by which to

Essay 25: *The Dangers of Subjectivism*

gauge our "advances" in moral behavior, how do we know that they are, indeed, advances? If you are only judging one set of subjective values against another set of subjective values, how can you tell if one is better than another? There must be a goal you are striving for, an objective universal norm that all men agree upon. If there is not, then there is no way of knowing if you are making progress or not. The very fact that we can compare ethical systems, and believe that one is better than another, necessitates an external, objective sense of what moral behavior should look like, and what to strive for.

This logical fallacy also demonstrates the danger of moral subjectivism. Without an objective norm for morals, then we are left with nothing more than subjective, arbitrary assertions of fallible human beings. And since we have no objective criteria for judging morals then one moral system is just as legitimate as another. Without the law of nature, the objective moral standard that comes from God Himself, you cannot rightfully critique one ethos as better or worse than another. You are left with having to approve of the morals of Adolf Hitler just as much as you would approve of the morals of Martin Luther King. If subjective experience and personal discovery is your only guide, then the Nazi death camps were as legitimately moral as the American Civil Rights movement. You cannot have it both ways. You cannot appeal to a higher morality if there is no objective, absolute standard by which to judge that there even is a higher morality.

There is another very dangerous aspect to subjectivism. Lewis points out that if there is no natural law, i.e., an objective standard for morality, then some person or persons have to become the legislators of moral standards for a society. Again, fallible people determine morality—and this is very perilous indeed. When we accept that there is an absolute right and wrong, and that our understanding of this comes from God, then there is a yardstick for behavior that everyone equally must follow. This applies to each member of society, no matter how high or how low. King and slave alike must follow the same moral code. However, when morals are subjective and arbitrary, determined by human lawgivers, then tyranny and oppression are likely to follow.

Witness what has happened in societies which have rejected the laws of nature (and of God) and set up their own ethical value systems. We saw this happen in Nazism and Fascism. We have seen (and still see) it happen in Communist societies. Consider the situation of a common soldier, he could be an SS guard at Dachau or a member of the Korean People's Army in North Korea. Let's say he is ordered to shoot an obviously innocent prisoner. He may find the act personally reprehensible (natural law does exist). However, he dutifully follows his orders. And he justifies it in his own mind because his action is "morally" consistent with the ethical values of his society. He kills an "enemy of the state" because the Fuhrer (or Eternal President, the specific country or title hardly matters) has deemed this a "good thing." In fact, the subjective moral code of his society will actually honor him for the murder of an innocent citizen.

Of course, we recoil at such a scenario. And rightfully so. We have been conditioned to think in moral terms that were originally soundly rooted in a Judeo-Christian ethic, an ethos which accepts as a basic premise that there is an objective, absolute natural law. As a matter of fact, not only our personal moral sense, but our entire system of democracy and our beliefs about liberty are founded in this reality. And without this objective moral code, there would be no freedom in our society. Notice what Lewis says in this regard: "The very idea of freedom presupposes some objective moral law which overarches rulers and ruled alike. Subjectivism about values is eternally incompatible with democracy. We and our rulers are of

Essay 25: *The Dangers of Subjectivism*

one kind only so long as we are subject to one law. But there is no Law of Nature, the ethos of any society is the creation of its rulers, educators, and conditioners; and every creator stands above and outside his own creation."

Here we see the great danger of subjectivism. It appears to give freedom of thought and expression. However, it actually engenders the opposite. It becomes the vehicle of control and oppression. We can illustrate this easily enough. Consider the current attitude about sexual morality in this country. At one time our sexual ethics were grounded in the Bible and natural law. Sexual activity was deemed moral and good if it occurred within the sacred confines of marriage, and a married state between one man and one woman. But as a society we have largely rejected this moral code. Now, anything and everything goes! And we are all supposed to accept this new morality—and not just accept but approve and commend it.

So where does this leave us? If you are part of the minority of Americans who still believe that adultery, fornication and homosexuality are immoral and indecent, then the culture at large condemns you. You are viewed as judgmental, bigoted, and narrow-minded. You are a hate-monger. You are unloving and unkind. In fact (they say), you are "immoral." And you are immoral to the point that you are also criminal. If you do not accept the morality of people who are adulterers, fornicators or homosexuals and you act on your convictions, you may be prosecuted for discrimination, or even a hate crime. (Are we not seeing this occur, and ever more frequently?) Do you see what has happened? Those who are immoral (according to natural law and objective norms) are now perceived as being on the "moral" high ground. And those who are truly virtuous and moral are deemed "immoral" and criminal. Rejection of the objective moral standards of our society has now resulted in the criminalization of those who hold to that traditional morality. And so to be a moral person in our society, especially if you are a Christian, becomes increasingly risky and perilous.

Now do you understand why we say that subjectivism is dangerous? It is a plague on personal moral behavior. Certainly. But the plague has infected the very life's blood of the entire culture. We may legitimately ask, can we continue to exist as a society if the plague continues?

Topical Guide to Essays

This collection of essays covers a wide variety of subjects. The purpose of this guide is to assist you, the reader, in selecting particular subjects. The numbers in the right hand column refer to the relevant essays as numbered in this book.

TOPIC	ESSAY
Astronomy	2, 10
Atheism	20, 21
Bible, Reliability	5, 10, 16
Christ	2, 5
Doctrine, Biblical	1, 11, 12, 14
Eastern Religion	19, 23
Education	1, 6, 19
Emergent Church	25

Environmentalism	3, 15
Evil	4, 16, 20, 21, 23
Evolution	3, 6, 10, 13, 15, 16
Evolution, Theistic	16
God	1, 2, 11, 12, 14, 20, 21
History	6, 22
Holines	1, 7, 18
Human Nature	2, 3, 4, 6, 16, 17, 19
Idolatry	11
Knowledge	1, 24
Love	12, 14, 20, 21
Missions & Evangelism	5
Morality & Immorality	3, 4, 7, 8, 9, 15, 17, 18, 23, 25
Naturalism	15, 17, 19
Niceness	9, 22
The Occult	19, 23
Philosophy	24
Postmodernism	18, 23
Reason	17, 24
Rule of Law	8
Salvation	5, 12
Science & Scientism	2, 10, 13, 17, 19
Sovereignty of God	20, 21
Sin	1, 4, 16, 20, 22
Subjectivism/Relativism	8, 23, 25
Theology	1, 11, 14
Trinity	12
Truth	9, 22, 23, 25
Value, Determining	2, 15
Worldview	10, 17, 18, 19, 24, 25

The Ministry of ANM

**ANM Publications is a ministry initiative of
Advancing Native Missions**

Advancing Native Missions (ANM) is a U.S.-based Christian missions agency. However, unlike many such agencies that are involved in sending missionaries from America to other places around the world, ANM works with indigenous missionaries. Indigenous (or native) missionaries are Christian workers who minister within their own sphere of influence proclaiming the Gospel of Jesus Christ to their own people. ANM then works to connect Christians in America with these brothers and sisters, to equip and encourage them. Our goal is to build relationships of love and trust between indigenous missionaries and North American individuals and churches. In this way, the entire body of Christ becomes involved in completing the Great Commission. **"And this gospel of**

the kingdom shall be preached in all the world as a witness to all nations, and then the end shall come" (Matthew 24:14).

If you would like to know how you can become an effective coworker with native missionaries to reach the unreached for Jesus Christ, contact ANM at contact@AdvancingNativeMissions.com, call us at 540-456-7111, or visit our website: www.AdvancingNativeMissions.com.

www.ingramcontent.com/pod-product-compliance
Lightning Source LLC
Chambersburg PA
CBHW051803040426
42446CB00007B/488